Beijing Tourism Manual

Mier W. Wang

China Travel & Tourism Press

Welcome to Beijing!
欢迎来北京！

Enjoy your Stay!

— Nick. Chen
陈亮熹，

Foreword

Beijing Tourism Manual is a comprehensive English guide for travels in Beijing. This book not only includes the primary historic tourist attractions, it devotes specific attention to scenic hotspots and numerous others, such as shopping, residence, dining, nightlife, and many more. In addition, the guide includes elaborate pictures, maps, and detailed descriptions of the Beijing area, offering readers insightful graphics. The *Beijing Tourism Manual* is uniquely one of the few articles on the bookshelf with a specific chapter completely dedicated to the 2008 Olympics.

Showing tremendous interest in China's heritage, Mier W. Wang is a high school student from the State of Michigan, the United States. Spending summers in China, Mier explores every corner of Beijing and familiarizes himself with the cultural and historic elements of the capital. Mier's book, without a doubt, is an exceptional accomplishment and experience for this youth, and in the days to come, I'm sure Mier's work will receive high graces from his readers. This young author will only continue to grow and mature, as this book merely foreshadows the extraordinary potential in this teenager.

Huang Ping
Consul General of
the People's Republic of China
in Chicago

Foreword

This fall of 2008, I will begin my fourth consecutive school year as Mier W. Wang's French teacher at Portage Central High School, located in Portage, Michigan in the Midwest region of the United States of America. I am honored that Mier has asked me to be part of this book that he has written Beijing located half way across the world and not even related to the subject matter of French for that matter. Nevertheless, by inviting me to join this next literary adventure with him, I strongly encourage, commend, and support Mier without hesitance. I personally look forward to witnessing Mier seize this opportunity to see for himself what it's like to be a young and successful writer and how far dreams and ambitions can guide us in our lifetimes and beyond.

Mier makes his teachers and family prouder than we probably should be. I must say that I am impressed of who Mier has become in the matter of the years in which I have known him. The following set of points about Mier comes from the teacher's voice within me.

- Mier was never asked to take on this ambitious assignment. When he chose to write this travel guide, he already had an exceptionally full schedule of course work, music performances, tennis practice, and other family obligations; all of which are priority before just being able to hang out with friends.
- Last summer when Mier was organizing himself to write this book while soaking up the sights and sounds of Beijing first-hand, he recognized the profound cultural and social impact a country experiences in terms of preparation upon being selected to host of the Olympic Games. He

also saw the opportunity being offered by writing about a city that is soon to be and forever will remain in the world's spotlight.

- Mier embraces his cultural heritage rather than ignores it in order to fit in. He is proud of his Chinese roots, and by writing this travel guide, he has invited others to become aware of what a town of over 5,000 years of history can offer.

I consider this guide to Beijing as a far-from-small-task that goes beyond most reasonable expectations and abilities of a down-to-earth 16-year-old adolescent who is born into a Chinese family but spent his youth in Japan, Canada, and the United States. Mier W. Wang has so eloquently described and captured the spirit of China's capital as seen, smelt, felt, heard, and tasted from a world traveler's perspective.

To Mier, I'm looking forward to working with you next year but in the long term may you forever continue to bloom wherever you are planted, hence granting you and yours a lifetime full of success and happiness. Grow and be well.

Sara G. Heil

Madame Sara Heil

Fellow avid world-traveler and Teacher of World Language

Preface

The capital of the People's Republic of China is one of the world's most diverse cities. Surviving over 5000 years of history, it is now complemented with (what I liked to call) "an economy on steroids" making it the most attractive location for people to see in China.

Spread all across Beijing, the numerous attractions give more than enough reasons to explain why Beijing is hosting the 2008 Olympics. Massive construction projects have changed the landscape, and the political, economic, cultural and communication centers of the country have prepared themselves for one of the greatest events in history.

Stepping out of Capital Airport in Beijing, I watched as the crowded road flooded with more and more ambitious taxi drivers. As I took more time to observe the Beijing atmosphere, the fast-pace market and the dreadful driving practices showed me that I wasn't in Kansas anymore.

After an entire summer exploring the capital, the city proved to be a lot more tireless than tourists might think. I remember how I was instantly flabbergasted by the opening of the plane doors; the outside air filled the airplane cabin, and I said to myself "Man is this place HOT!"

This Beijing Handbook will help readers to fully intake the numerous sites that Beijing has to offer. Whether you intend on visiting The Forbidden City or sampling genuine Chinese cuisine, this handbook will reveal many of the cultural differences that commonly shock tourists.

by Mier W. Wang
On September, 2007,
in Portage, Michigan, USA

Contents

Contents

Contents

Chapter 1

About Beijing

Beijing is the capital of the People's Republic of China. This metropolis is the second largest city in the country next to Shanghai, and it is the political, economic, educational, and cultural center of China.

1-1 Geography

As a tourist, the responsibility rests on your shoulders to know at least the fundamentals to the location of where you are traveling; that makes it my responsibility as your guide to tell you some basics to the geographic location of Beijing. So here we go...

Beijing is located in China, on the West coast of the Pacific Ocean. The Yanshan Mountains surround the capital in the North, East, and West side (61% of the city is occupied by mountainous terrain), while Yongding River flows in the South. As you can see, tourists can easily enjoy the luscious mountainside views of Beijing one day and meet the roaring seas the next; this is a perfect location for those who enjoy "all-in-one" vacations.

Beijing is 39% flat land and the other 61% is quite mountainous. The center of the city is situated at 39°56' North Latitude and 116°20' East Longitude. For those looking for fascinating facts, Beijing is situated approximately the same latitude as Philadelphia of the United States and Madrid of Spain!

1-2 Climate

One of the most important tips that I can give you about the climate is to DRESS ACCORDINGLY. Beijing is full of surprises when it comes to the weather, especially for tourists.

Winter

The air in Beijing during winter is extremely dry. For those who aren't afraid of the cold, winter can be a very fascinating time to explore the city. Many layers of clothing are highly recommended to fend off the bitingly cold winds.

Spring

The spring in Beijing is very brief and dry. For tourists who are vacationing during this season, the thing to pay most attention to is what the Chinese like to call "Yellow Wind." Beijing springs are known to be EXTREMELY DUSTY. High winds carry sand particles all the way from the Gobi Desert to pester people walking outside. Today, many tree-planting renovations have commenced to minimize the effects of these winds.

Summer

The summer temperatures in Beijing can be scorching. Other than light clothing, it's hard to prepare for this type of condition, so the best advice would be to bring a lot of sunscreen and bug spray (there can be a lot of mosquitoes). Something else to look out for is the warm and humid monsoon winds blowing in from the southeast: this is what brings in most of Beijing's annual precipitation. The capital offers a healthy dose of heavy thundershowers especially in the afternoons; don't forget your umbrella!

Autumn

Beijing's autumn is the most comfortable time to visit. With only a little precipitation, the climate is neither too dry nor too humid, making it just right.

Here's a chart for visual learners

	Jan	Feb	Mar	Apr	May	Jun
High	34˚F 1℃	39˚F 4℃	52˚F 11℃	70˚F 21℃	81˚F 27℃	88˚F 31℃
Low	14˚F -10℃	18˚F -8℃	30˚F -1℃	45˚F 7℃	55˚F 13℃	64˚F 18℃
	Jul	**Aug**	**Sep**	**Oct**	**Nov**	**Dec**
High	88˚F 31℃	86˚F 30℃	79˚F 26℃	68˚F 20℃	48˚F 9℃	37˚F 3℃
Low	70˚F 21℃	68˚F 20℃	57˚F 14℃	43˚F 6℃	28˚F -2℃	18˚F -8℃

1-3 Population and Ethnicity

One of the eye-openers for an average tourist is the uncountable number of people walking on the streets of Beijing everyday. Here's some information about the city's population.

The actual city is almost 17,000 sq. km, and its boundaries extend up to 80 km. Over fifteen million people occupy this large area with plentiful stores, delicious restaurants, and arrays of services for your convenience.

- Beijing's population grew to fifteen million at 2005, almost four times the census in 1949.
- Approximately, 50,000 newborns are born each year.
- Beijing has 11.8 million permanent residents and over 3 million transient populations.
- The population of people who use public transportation is close to four million.
- China's 56 ethnic groups are all recognized in Beijing. The majority (96.5%) of the city's population is of the Han ethnic group. About 300,000 people of the population account for the other 55 minorities.

1-4 Area and Districts

The Municipality of Beijing governs a total of 16 urban districts and 2 rural counties:

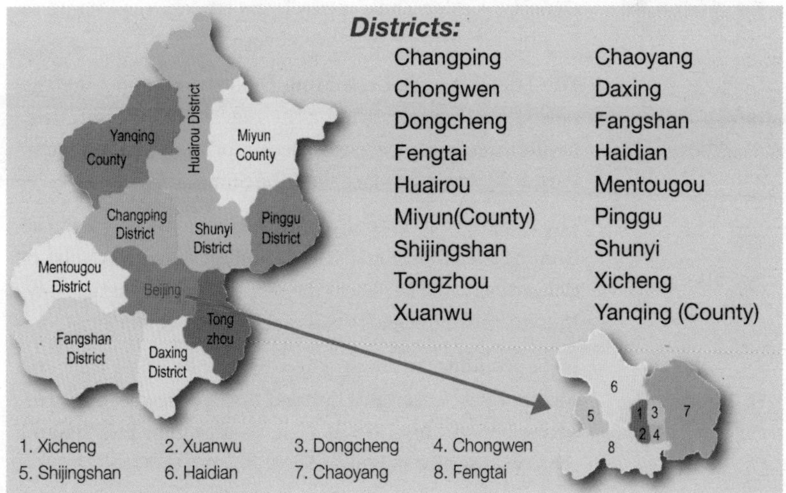

1-5 History of Beijing

As early as 400,000 years ago	The first caveman born in China was nicknamed the "Peking Man." He lived in Zhoukoudian, in the southwestern suburbs of Beijing.
1045 B.C –	A small town was formed southwest of present day Beijing. It was named JI, but later was renamed YAN. It became a major city in northern China. The recorded history of Beijing as a city can date back to more than 3,000 years ago.
907 –	Qidan people founded the Liao Dynasty. They occupied and established Beijing, which was renamed as "Jiuzhou,"
1153 –	Jin Dynasty, which controlled North China, chose Beijing as the official capital, naming it "Jin Zhong Du".
1215 –	Jin Zhong Du fell to Mongolian warlord Genghis Khan during the Mongolian campaign to build a vast empire. After a seven-year siege, the city was destroyed. Genghis Khan's grandson Kublai Khan rebuilt the city in 1267 to replace Jin Zhong Du and named it Dadu. By 1279, Kublai had conquered all of China, becoming the ruler of largest country in history. This era is known as the Yuan Dynasty (1279-1368).
1368 –	Zhu Yuanzhang led an uprising against the Mongol Empire and seized Khan's great city. This began the Ming Dynasty. Under Zhu's control, the city changed name to Beiping – meaning "Northern Peace."
1644 –	The Manchu ended the Ming Dynasty, establishing the new Qing Dynasty. Under the new rulers, Beijing was modernized with the construction of the Yuanmingyuan Park (Old Summer Place) and the Summer Place.
1911 –	The Qing Dynasty finally collapsed in 1911. In 1928, the Nanjing-based nationalist government of the Republic of China designated Beijing as the Beiping Special Municipality. In 1930, the municipality was renamed as Beiping City.
1949 –	In September 27, 1949, the Chinese People's Political consultative Conference decided that the newborn People' s Republic of China would base its capital in Beiping and renamed the city as Beijing.

1-6 Beijing Culture

Because of China's extended history, it is a treasure cave of cultural heritage and legendary artifacts. In addition to the various cultures, Beijing is also rich in religion. All around Beijing, adorned temples reveal ancient religious practices of the Chinese civilization. But of course, Beijing is also filled with magnificent architectural feats, such as the Forbidden City, Ming Tombs, the Great Wall, and even Hutongs. The many landmarks in Beijing offer more than enough for tourists to fill a day's schedule. But, these unbelievable accomplishments reveal only a sample of Beijing's countless wonders. Beijing, in fact, also holds art at high-esteem as well. Tourists frequently visit popular theater houses to enjoy unique Beijing operas, acrobatic shows, and traditional Chinese dramas. While preserving historic remnants, Beijing persistently undergoes change and renovation, making it a different city everyday.

1-7 Beijing City Flowers and Trees

Chrysanthemum

Chinese rose

Guohuai

Oriental Arborvitae

With thousands of years of history, Beijing also has thousands of tourist attractions. From arduous hikes on the Great Wall to the glorious memories in the Forbidden City, Beijing has got them all. Many of these sites are on the prestigious list of the United Nations' World Culture Heritage Sites, which shows Beijing's role as a tourist magnet. Bustling with economic revolutions and constantly feeding hungry people, Beijing offers a collection of sites that will bring unforgettable experiences to picture-perfect sceneries. Also offering a taste of the Chinese culture and history, Beijing's numerous tourist hot spots are have-to-see stops on your itinerary.

Chapter 2

Tourist Attractions

2-1

Forbidden City

Forming the heart of Beijing, the Forbidden City, or Gugong in Chinese, has survived the rule of 24 emperors, lasting over 500 years. All the way until 1924 (the royal family was removed that year), this was the imperial palace where emperors and governments wrote history and made national decisions. During the 500 years, officials forbade the public from entering Gugong, which led to its

The Forbidden City's Full View take from Jingshan Park

Wumen(Meridian Gate)

name the "Forbidden City." Taking 15 years and millions of workers to complete, the gigantic Gugong was built with exactly 9,999 rooms (10,000 being a sacred number only to be used by gods), and it offered housing to almost everyone, including the imperial family, servants, officials, consorts, concubines, eunuchs, and many more.

Taihedian (Hall of Supreme Harmony)

This palatial complex has suffered through many losses. First, Japanese troops controlled Gugong for a duration of time, leading to unforeseen damages and losses. Then on the eve of Communist victory, defeated Kuomintang members transported countless crates of relics and artifacts to Taiwan, where today, these historic goods are exhibited in Taipei's National Palace Museum. Despite these surviving remnants, many rare books, paintings, calligraphy, and other historic valuables have been lost throughout Gugong's long history.

Baohedian

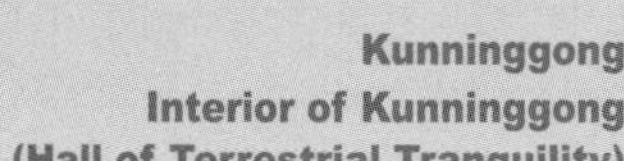

Kunninggong
Interior of Kunninggong
(Hall of Terrestrial Tranquility)

Zhonghedian & Baohedian
(Hall of Complete Harmony)
(Hall of Preserving Harmony)

Attractions List in Gugong

- Wumen (Meridian Gate) – This is the colossal south entrance of the Forbidden City. It is divided into five archways, which people can walk through. Back in imperial times, the center archway was purely restricted for the Emperor himself.
- Taihedian (Hall of Supreme Harmony) – This Hall is the largest building in the Forbidden City and also the largest wooden structure in all of China. It functioned as the throne hall where major occasions, such as Chinese New Year and enthronement, took place.
- Zhonghedian (Hall of Complete Harmony) – The Hall of Complete Harmony is one of the three outer halls in Forbidden City. Square in shape, this hall is where Emperors used to rest and prepare himself before large events and ceremonies.
- Baohedian (Hall of Preserving Harmony) – The Hall of Preserving Harmony is the third outer hall, where ceremonial rehearsals and the imperial examination took place. There is a throne located here that is similar, yet smaller, than the one in the Hall of Supreme Harmony.
- Qianqinggong (Palace of Heavenly Peace) – This was the residential housing for the emperor during the Ming and early Qing Dynasty. Later, this building was used for receiving foreign ambassadors.

- Jiaotaidian (Hall of Union and Peace) - Located next to the Palace of Heavenly Peace, The Hall of Union and Peace houses the 25 Imperial seals of the Qing Dynasty .
- Kunninggong (Hall of Terrestrial Tranquility) – This hall is where the empresses of the Ming Dynasty lived. You can recognize this building because it is completely painted in red.
- Imperial Garden – This is the luscious garden for the Imperial family to enjoy.
- Office of Privy Council – This office was originally built as the room where Emperors dealt with military and political affairs.
- Zhenfei's Well – In 1900, this was the well where Empress Dowager Cixi forced Concubine Zhenfei to drown. Forces of the Eight Allied Power were approaching the doors of Beijing, and instead of escaping, Zhenfei was forced to die. Zhenfei was emperor Guang Xu's favorite concubine.

Imperial Garden (Yu Hua Yuan)

Interior of Baohedian

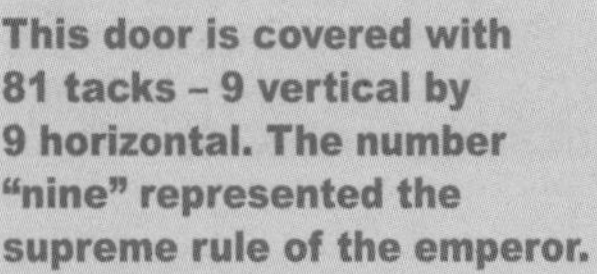

This door is covered with 81 tacks – 9 vertical by 9 horizontal. The number "nine" represented the supreme rule of the emperor.

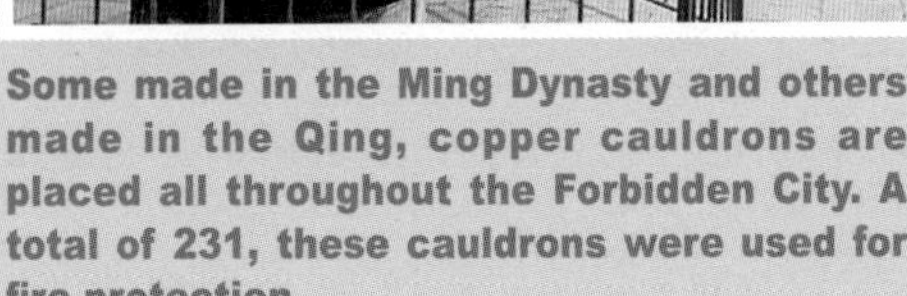

Some made in the Ming Dynasty and others made in the Qing, copper cauldrons are placed all throughout the Forbidden City. A total of 231, these cauldrons were used for fire protection.

This is Concubine Zhenfei's Well. Zhenfei was the emperor's favorite concubine. She was forced to jump into this well and commit suicide by Empress Dowager Cixi in 1900.

Visitor Check List

✉	4 Jingshan Qianjie, Dongcheng District
🚌	101, 103, 109, 111, 120, 126, 726, 728, 810, 814, 846, at Gugong Station; 1, 2, 4, 10, 20, 22, 52, 54, 57, 120, 802 at Tian'anmen Station or Zhongshan Park Station; Subway Line 1 at Tian'anmen Station
🕒	8:30 to 17:00; Daily
☎	86-10-6153 2255
💰	40 RMB (Nov.1-Mar.31); 60 RMB (Apr.1-Oct. 31) The Clock & Watch Museum and Treasure House cost additional 10 RMB each.
⏱	1-3hours (Recommended time for a visit)

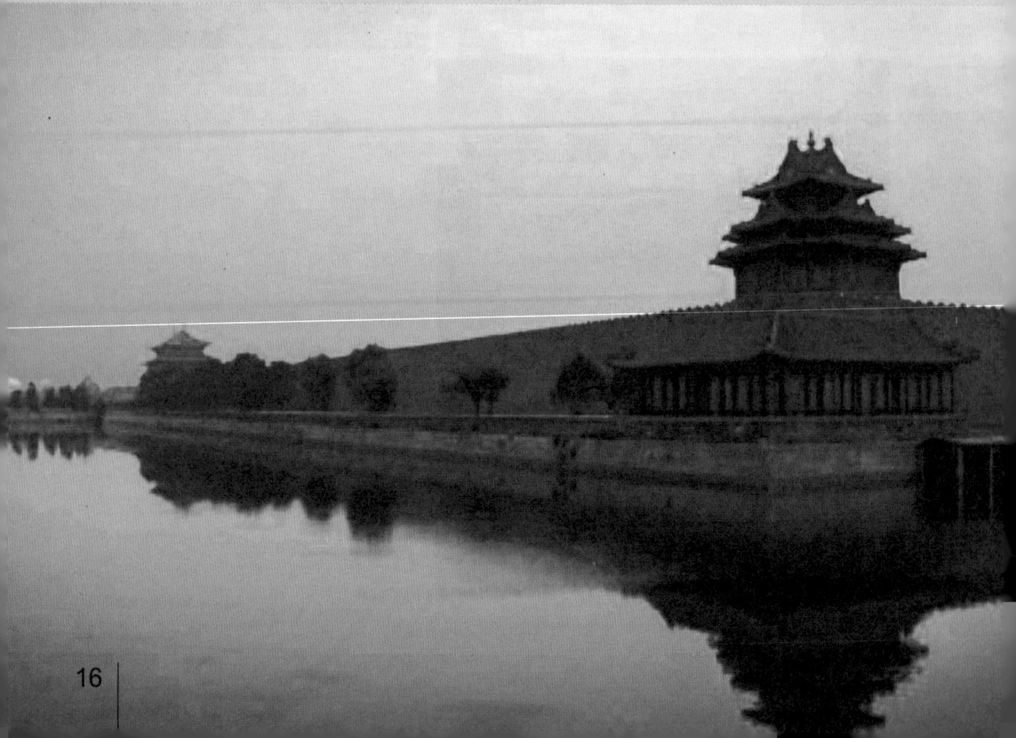

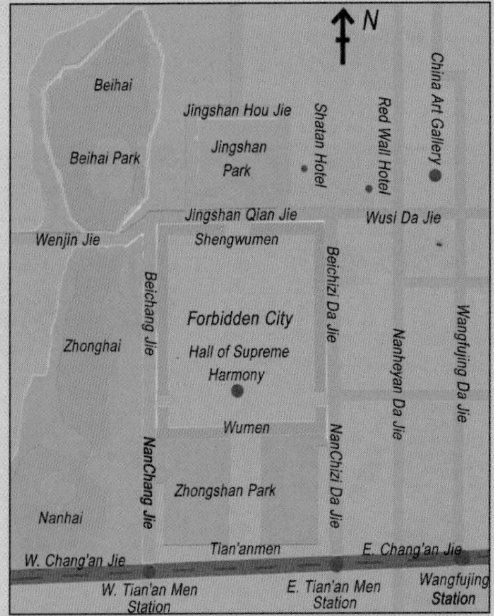

The Forbidden City is Located in the Center of Beijing City

The Man-made Moat Guarding the Forbidden City

2-2

Temple of Heaven

Heading southeast of Beijing, tourists can dedicate some vacation time to the Temple of Heaven, also known as Tiantan Park. The temple was built from 1406 to 1420 under Emperor Yongle of Ming Dynasty. This place was where a total of twenty-two Ming and Qing emperors worshipped heaven and prayed for good harvests. In 1915, Yuan Shikai held the last event of heaven worship. Having housed over six hundred celebrations, the Temple of Heaven is the world's largest architectural complex for rituals and worship to heaven.

Yuanqiutan

The Temple of Heaven has a unique architectural design; it is divided into an inner altar and an outer altar. The main buildings of the temple lie at the south and north ends of the central axis line of the inner altar, and tourists usually enter from the south.

The Yuanqiutan (Circular Mound Altar) is where emperors offered sacrifice to Heaven on the day of the Winter Solstice every year. Located in the southern region, this ancient altar is a marble structure, 5.7 meters high and 23 meters in diameter.

The Huangqiongyu (Imperial Vault of Heaven) is a circular temple with conic roof, which is decorated with glazed tiles and adorned with an elaborate ball. This temple houses many tablets of emperors.

The Qiniandian (Hall of Prayer for Good Harvests) is located in the northern sector of the park. Emperors came to this temple to offer sacrificed animals and burn incense sticks to pray for fruitful harvest. Qiniandian (Hall of Prayer for Good

Huangqiongyu

Interior of Huangqiongyu

Harvests) is frequently referred to as the symbol of the Temple of Heaven.

The Temple of Heaven is a medley of ancient Chinese beliefs, including music, garden, technology, calendar, painting, and architecture. However, the most remarkable significance of the Temple of Heaven is probably the union of ceremonial purposes and geometry.

According to Chinese belief, Heaven is round and Earth is

Front Gate of Zhaigong

square. The northern part of temple is semicircular symbolizing the heavens, and the southern part is square symbolizing the Earth. The northern part is higher than the southern part.

Additionally, Zhaigong (Hall of Abstinence) is another popular attraction. This is where emperors prepared himself in abstinence before the ceremonies began. Shenyueshu (Divine Music Hall) is the imperial organization managing the performances during ceremonies.

Nine-Dragon Cypress

The Echo Wall

Danbiqiao (Red Stairway Bridge) is 360 meters long and 30 meters wide, and travels from the south to the north of the Temple of Heaven.

Long Corridor

The map of Temple of Heaven:

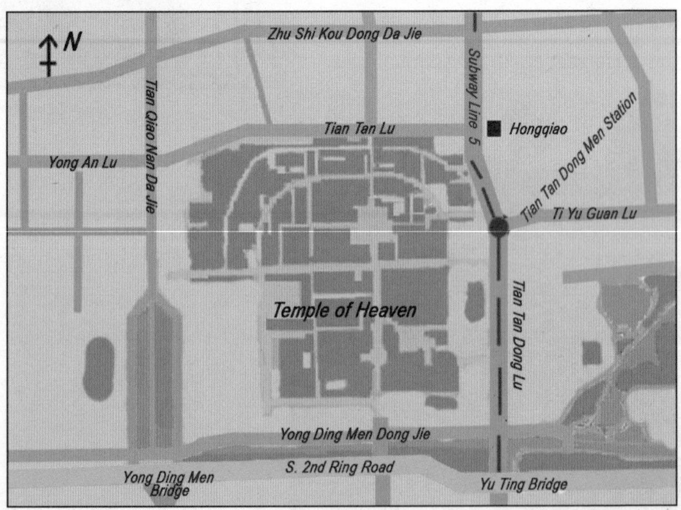

Visitor Check List

✉	A1 Tiantan Dong Lu, Chongwen District
🚌	2, 6, 15, 16, 17, 20, 34, 35, 36, 43, 45, 54, 60,106,110,116,120,122, 610, 684, 685, 723, 800, 803, 814, 822, 958
🕒	6:00 am-10:00 pm; Daily
☎	86-10-6702-8866
💰	15 RMB (ordinary ticket); 35 RMB (inclusive ticket) (Nov.-Mar.); 10 RMB (ordinary ticket);30 RMB (inclusive ticket) (Apr.-Oct.)
⏱	1.5 hours (Recommended time for a visit time)

2-3 Great Wall

The Great Wall of China, translated from "Wan Li Chang Cheng," is unquestionably a have-to-see attraction for all tourists around the world. Not only is the Great Wall the Eighth Wonder of the World, it is a symbol of China that holds various chapters of history. Originally built as a means of fortification, it has become one of the most popular tourist attractions in China. Stretching over 6,400 kilometers, the walls snake across high mountains and vast deserts, from Shanhai guan (山海关) in the east to Jiayu guan (嘉峪关) in the west.

Construction of the Great Wall started during the era of the Warring States (around 221 BC); the first emperor of the Qin Dynasty united seven separate states into one joint nation, which eventually developed into what we know today as China. In order to defend the aggression approaching from the north, the emperor Qin Shihuang (秦始皇) called on over one million workers, which at that time corresponded to one fifth of the entire population, to link the separated wall up and rebuild, reinforce, and extend them complete the fortification walls. Over 180 million cubic meters of

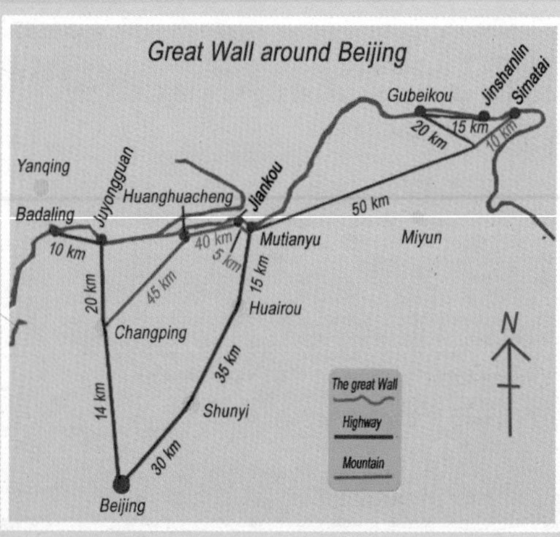

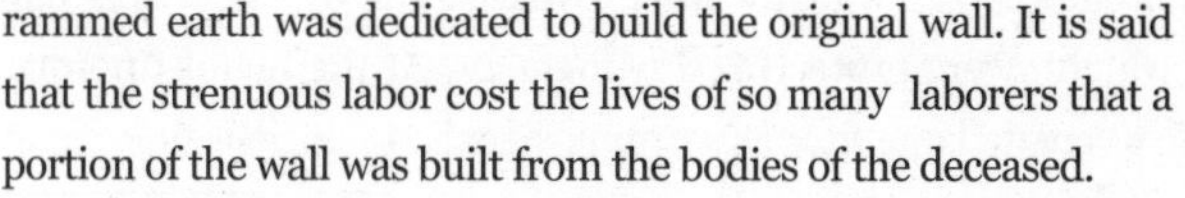

rammed earth was dedicated to build the original wall. It is said that the strenuous labor cost the lives of so many laborers that a portion of the wall was built from the bodies of the deceased.

The wall was extensively renovated during the Ming Dynasty in the 16th century. This time, cannons and towers were added, and the overall length was also enlarged. Not only that, most of the wall was remade with bricks and stones.

Over 600 miles of the Great Wall swerves through Beijing, and it is split into four unique sections, each with an exceptional quality for tourists to enjoy. Here are the four portions: the popular Badaling（八达岭）, the adventurous Simatai（司马台）, the admired Mutianyu（慕田峪）, and the breathtaking Juyongguan（居庸关）.

Badaling （八达岭）

Located in Yanqing County, Badaling is the most popular section of the Great Wall for local folks and tourists alike. Around 44 miles northwest of Beijing, Badaling is a relatively nearby attraction for anyone looking for an exciting experience. At an elevation of 1000 meters, Badaling is divided into the Gentlemen's Slope in the South and the Lady's slope in the North. The Lady's Slope is very crowded, while the Gentlemen's Slope is less populated due to the steep slopes. Offering numerous opportunities for a Kodak moment, Badaling

Great Wall was built around 1505 during the Ming Dynasty. The wall is strategically located and has 19 watchtowers protecting Juyongguan. At the highest points, platforms were made to create large fires as warning signals. In ancient times, one fire with one smoke meant that there were about 100 enemy soldiers, while two fires with two smokes meant about 500. Three fires with three smoke meant that 1,000

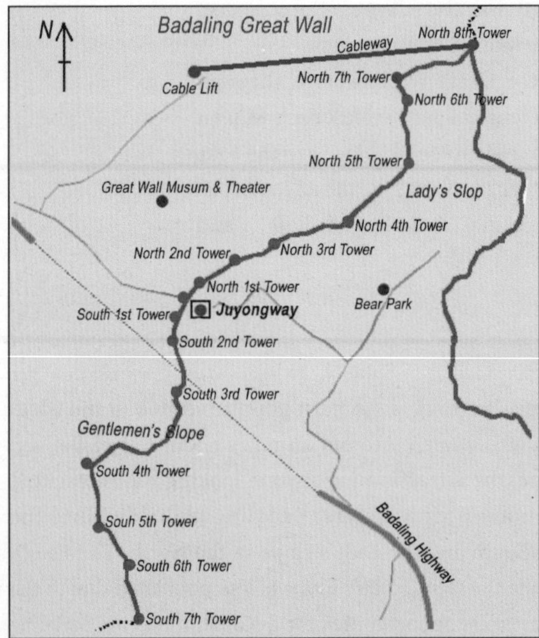

men were approaching. With this system, soldiers could not only be warned, they could be armed with information concerning the enemy. Badaling averages 7.5 meters high, 6.5 meters wide at the base, and 5.8 meters wide at the top. This platform is wide enough for five horses or ten soldiers to travel side by side.

Although this section is popular amongst sightseeing vacations, do not

Visitor Check List

	Yanqing County
	919(from Deshengmen; Depart between 6:00-15:00;12CNY; Depart every 5 minuts)
	From Xizhimen; Depart at 7:30 and back from Badaling at 15:20;4.5CNY
	8:00 am to 6:30 pm; Daily
	86-10-6912-1737(1017);86-10-8119-1011
	45 RMB (Cableway 60 RMB)
	2-4 hours (Recommended time for a visit time)

underestimate the steepness of Badaling; there are angles that can make your legs go soft.

In 1990, the Great Wall Circle Vision Theater was opened to offer a more education experience for people. The 360-degree amphitheater shows 15-minute long films about the Great Wall - Eighth Wonder of the World.

Simatai (司马台)

Simatai is incontestably the marvel of the Great Wall available to tourists. People say that the Great Wall is the greatest structure of China, but Simatai is the best of the Great Wall. A well-known proverb of the Chinese states "He who hasn't climbed Simatai is not a true man." The validity of this statement might be questionable, but anyone who completely walks Simatai will remember the experience forever; there are no words to describe the pleasure of completing this course. This portion of the wall is located slightly northeast of Miyun County in Gubeikou Town. If you are looking for a nicely unspoiled and natural display, Simatai is the place to go.

Simatai is nicknamed the "obstacle-wall;" It's easy to say that

this wall will be a challenge. Having slopes with an incline up to 70 degrees, Simatai will require you to have both hands free, a nice pair of running shoes as well as a camera to immortalize this event. This section of the wall does not have many tourists like Badaling because of the rigorous course, so those looking for an opportunity to take nature pictures will find it here. Simatai is known for its countless challenges, and there have been many tourist trappings as well. Hey, it's not that easy to pass a narrow footpath with a 500-meter drop.

Here's a little background information about the wall. Simatai dates back to the Ming Dynasty when renovations created 35 watch towers. The Wall is separated into an eastern and western part by a river and valley. The western part is gently sloped and is accompanied by 20 well-preserved watchtowers. The eastern part is much more precipitous and has 15 watchtowers scattered along the wall. These

towers are closely spaced and provide spectacular views of the mountains, rugged terrain, cliffs, and kilometer-high peaks. The main attractions in the east include Watching Beijing Tower, Fairy Tower, Heavenly Ladder and Sky Bridge.

Tourists can choose between two different routes when traveling to Simatai. The most popular pathway is a 12-kilometer hike along Jinshanling to Simatai. Although the actual distance is not intimidating, the rough terrain makes this hike four to five hours long. The entire workout at Simatai should take up the entire day, which includes the 2-hour travel between Simatai and Beijing.

Visitor Check List

✉	Gueikou Town, Miyun County
🚌	You 12 at Qianmen Jishan Center; Depart between 6:30-9:00 am; 100 RMB including admission fee 40 RMB
🕒	8:00 am to 17:00 pm; Daily
☎	86-10-6903-1051;86-10-6903-5022
💰	40 RMB (additional: Cableway: 50 RMB or 30 RMB for only one way; Tower express: 30 RMB or 20 RMB for one way; Slide plus boat: 35 RMB or boat only 10 RMB)
⏱	One day (Recommended time for a visit time)

Mutianyu (幕田峪)

Mutianyu is the second most popular location of the Great Wall next to Badaling. It is a little less than 100 miles away from Beijing in the Huairou District, and there are many transport buses that can take you there. There is a lot of vegetation around that area, and Mutianyu is just like Badaling with its amazing views. The watchtowers in this portion of the wall are unique compared to the other sections. Not only are there plentiful amounts of these sentries, the towers were placed in highly defensive positions. Mutianyu, mostly made of granite, offers one of the most breath-taking views as the wall snakes through the green ocean of beautiful plants and trees.

Visitor Check List

✉	Mutianyu Village, Huairou District
🚌	916 (Depart between 6:00-18:00 at Dongzhimen, 11 RMB, take about 2 hours to Huairou International conference Center, and then take a small bus to the Mutianyu Great Wall, 10 RMB)
🕒	8:00 am to 18:00 pm; Daily
☎	86-10-6162-6505;86-10-6162-6022
💰	35 RMB (additional: Cable car 50 RMB or 35 RMB for one way; Slide way: 55 RMB)
⏱	2-3hours (Recommended time for a visit time)

Juyongguan (居庸关)

Think of Juyongguan as more of a military castle than a wall. It was originally built in the fifth-century and was intensely renovated during the Ming Dynasty. It is a quiet attraction located in the Changping District, and it acted as a door to Beijing. Because of its position as an entrance, Juyongguan faced a more violent history than any other portion of the wall. The fortress has numerous watchtowers as well as uncountable beacon towers; tourists visiting the capital's guardian can enjoy the quiet, clean air and absorb the splendid views.

Travel

Visitor Check List

✉	Nankouzhen, Changping District
🚌	919 (Depart between 6:00-17:00 at Deshengmen, take about 2 hours to reach Juyongguan station, 10 RMB or At Subway line 13 Longze Station take bus No.20 to Juyongguan)
🕒	8:00 am to 17:00 pm; Daily
☎	86-10-6977-1665
💰	45 RMB
⏱	2-3hours (Recommended time for a visit time)

2-4

Summer Palace

Located 15 kilometers northwest of central Beijing, the Summer Palace has existed here for over 8 centuries. In the 18th century, Qing Dynasty Emperor Qianlong constructed the palace into the royal house that we know today. The royal family would take shelter here during the sweltering hot summer seasons. And the water would keep them cool. Later the Summer Palace was mostly associated with the Empress Dowager Cixi, who had the palace rebuilt twice. Once following its destruction by French and English troops in 1860, Empress Cixi diverted 30 million taels of silver, originally designated

for the Chinese navy Beiyang Fleet, into the reconstruction and enlargement of the Summer Palace (the Beiyang Fleet lost the Jiawu War in 1895).

Empress Cixi's second renovation took place after the Summer Palace was ransacked

Bull

Lion

Phoenix

Dragon

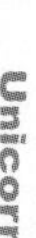

Unicorn

during the Boxer rebellion in 1900. The Eight-power Allied Forces took away everything valuable and destroyed the buildings. Cixi's government was, by this time, reduced to such financial shortages that it was unable to allot any money for restoration. Finally in 1924 when the last emperor Puyi was removed, the Summer Palace was open to the public. Since 1949, the government of New China has been funding to renovate most ramshackle buildings and scenic spots according to their original designs and their former grandeur.

Today the Summer palace is the

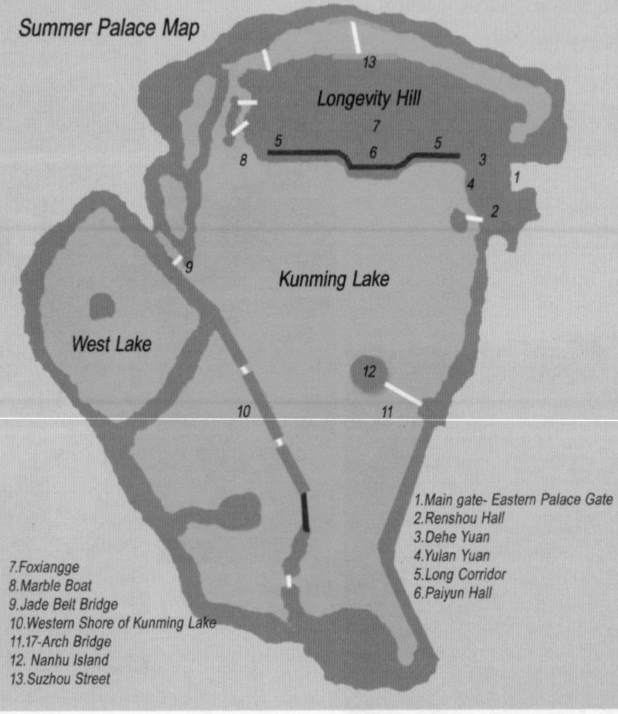

Summer Palace Map

Longevity Hill
Kunming Lake
West Lake

1.Main gate- Eastern Palace Gate
2.Renshou Hall
3.Dehe Yuan
4.Yulan Yuan
5.Long Corridor
6.Paiyun Hall
7.Foxiangge
8.Marble Boat
9.Jade Belt Bridge
10.Western Shore of Kunming Lake
11.17-Arch Bridge
12. Nanhu Island
13.Suzhou Street

loveliest imperial park in China. It occupies an area of 726.5 acres, and to walk along the entire shoreline of the man-made lake would take about 2 hours. In fact three quarters of the Summer Palace is made up of water. Like most imperial palaces in China, the Summer Palace is divided into three parts: halls for political affairs, living quarters, and religious buildings.

All very nice and full of tourists, the Summer Palace is not just an imperial vacation home; in fact, it is a nice example of classical Chinese garden architecture. Composed mainly of Longevity Hill and Kunming Lake, the Summer Palace is a unique combination of nature and architecture. Some attractions to enjoy include the Foxiangge, Long Corridor, the Marble Boat, The 17-Arch Bridge, Deheyuan Theater, and Suzhou Street...

If you have enough time, don't forget to bring a blanket and some food and drinks– there are loads of lovely places on the way for a nice picnic.

Visitor Check List

- Yiheyuan Lu & Kunminghu Lu, Haidian District
- 303, 330, 331, 332, 333, 346, 375, 394, 718, 737, 801, 808, ...
- 6:30 am-6:00 pm (Apr. - Oct.); 7:00 am - 5:00 pm (Nov. - Mar.); Daily
- 86-10-6288-1144
- 30 RMB (ordinary ticket) 60 RMB (inclusive ticket)
- 3 hours (Recommendated time for a visit time)

1. Marble Boat (石舫)

The Marble Boat is positioned at the west bank at the foot of Longevity Hill. Built in 1755, the hull of the boat measures 36 meters in length. It was originally used to have an awing of Chinese style but was burnt down by the French and English Troops in 1860. In 1893, the boat was rebuilt in a foreign style by Empress Dowager Cixi. Then in 1903, the Empress added a second level to the boat and decorated it with colorful pieces of glass. Empress Dowager Cixi often came to the Marble boat to enjoy some tea and the striking landscapes.

2. The Long Corridor（长廊）

The Long Corridor is in front of Longevity Hill, and it leads from the Yao Yue Men in the east, westwards along the northern shore of Kunming Lake to Shizhang Ting. The 728 meter-long corridor is divided into 273 sections and has over 14,000 traditional Chinese paintings inscribed on beams and crossbeams. Originally, the corridor was first built in 1750 by Emperor Qianlong. In 1860, the French-English Troops severely damaged the Long Corridor. It was finally rebuilt in 1886.

Inspired by the 14th century historical novel *Romance of the Three Kindoms*, this picture illustrates the vicious battle that took place between Zhang Fei and Ma Chao, who were two of the Five Tiger Generals in Shu Kingdom.

4. The 17-Arch Bridge (17 孔桥)

The 17-Arch Bridge is a 150-meter-long and 8-meter wide stone-made bridge, which was built in 1750. The bridge connects Octagonal Tower in the east and the South Lake Island in the south. There are a total of 544 lion-covered posts on the bridge.

4. Dehe (Virtuous Harmony) Theater (德和戏院)

This grand theater is located in Deheyuan. It is 21 meters tall and 17 meters wide with three floors. The performances could take place on all three floors at same time. Empress Cixi was a Chinese opera-fancier.

5. Foxiangge (Tower of Baddhist Incense) (佛香阁)

Over 40 meters tall, the Foxiangge was the biggest project in the palace. Looking out to the lake and palace, this pavilion, the symbol of the Summer Palace, can be seen on Kunminghu Lake.

6. Paiyun Dian (Hall of Dispelling Clouds) (排云殿)

Paiyundian was a temple specifically made to celebrate Empress Cixi's birthday.

7. Dayuanbaojing (大圆宝镜)

Empress Cixi's favorite horizontal inscribed board

8. *Jade Belt Bridge*（玉带桥）

9. *Parts of Longevily Hill*（万寿山）

10. Yannian Jing (延年井)

Cixi's Personal Water Well

11. Bronze Pavilion (铜亭)

12. Suzhou Street (苏州街)

2-5

Yuanmingyuan Park (Old Summer Palace)

Originally built during the 12th century, the foundations of the Yuanmingyuan Park (Old Summer Palace), also known as the "Garden of Perfect Brightness," was once the most extolled garden in the world. Emperors and royal family members would come to this location to enjoy the peaceful sway of trees as well as the gentle ripples of water. With an area of over 350 hectares (40 percent being water), this lovely vacation spot had over 140 scenic attractions and over 200 florid buildings making it the largest royal garden during that era.

Starting in 1709, major renovation feats were initiated under Qing Emperor Kangxi.

Throughout the 18th century, further generations of emperors contributed more and more to the garden. Emperor Qianlong, in one case, hired Jesuit architects to construct an interlocking-designed garden. Many sections of the Summer Palace were built in a European style that mirror structures of Versailles in France. The enormous royal garden is split into sections,

Old Summer Palace in Traditional Chinese Painting

each with its own unique attraction for tourists to view.

In the west is the main section called the "Garden of Perfect Brightness." In the south, tourists can walk around the "Ten-thousand Spring Garden." The most preserved artifact of the palace is located on the eastside; this section is called "Garden of Eternal Spring," and it accommodates the popular ruins of the European palaces.

Sadly, the majority of the Old Summer Palace was destroyed during the Second Opium War in 1860. British and French troops plumaged many buildings and demolished the treasured gardens. The Chinese government continues to preserve and protect the royal family's holiday spot, and despite the upsetting views of the garden's ruins, tourists still travel to the Old Summer Palace to enjoy the remade scenery and remember the nostalgic history.

Ruins of Old Summer Palace

Visitor Check List

✉	No. 28 Qinghua Xi Lu, Haidian District
🚌	331, 365, 432, 438, 498, 628, 664, 716, 726, 814, 982, ...
☎	7:00 am-7:00 pm (Apr. - Oct.); 7:00 am - 5:30 pm (Nov. - Mar.); Daily
🕒	86-10-6255-1488; 86-10-6254-3673
💰	10 RMB (ordinary ticket); 35 RMB (inclusive ticket)
⏱	1 hour (Recommended time for a visit time)

2-6 Ming Tombs (Shisanling)

Located in the Changping District, thirteen emperors of the Ming Dynasty peacefully lie in their majestic mausoleums. Known as the Ming Tombs – translated from "Shishanling," which literally means "thirteen tombs" – these magnificent graves are now not only the final resting grounds of Chinese royalty, they are extremely popular tourist attractions as well. Back in

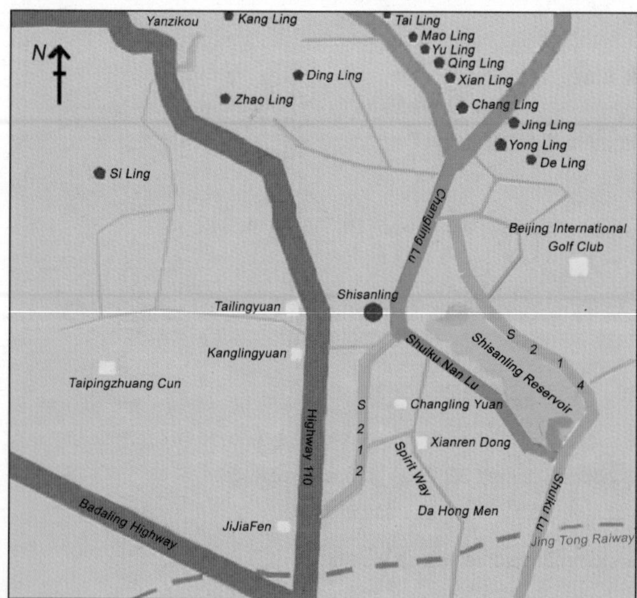

The Map of Ming Tombs

Ding Ling

the days of imperial rule, the death of an emperor was complemented with some interesting rituals. Also, many relics and artifacts – mostly apparels and ceremonial clothing – are enclosed in the tomb.

The Imperial Cemetery of the thirteen emperors covers 40 square kilometers. The only tomb that has been excavated is that of Emperor Wanli (万历) (1573-1619), which is called Ding Ling (定陵). Today, the public can climb down many flights of spiraling stairs to reach the deep, solemn grave. Listening to other people's quiet echoes, many tourists come to witness the numerous stone chambers, treasure trunks, and funerary belongings. According to historic documents, over half a million workers took six years to complete Ding Ling.

Two others, Changling (长陵) and Zhaoling (昭陵), are now open to the public. As the largest amongst all the tombs, Chang Ling is the other popular location of the Ming Tombs. It is the resting place of Emperor Yongle (永　乐) (1403-1424), and it is most renowned for the actual road that leads to the tomb. Known as the “Spirit Way” (神　路 -Shen Lu), the stone walkway is lined with hundreds of stone monuments and statues. These statues come in diverse shapes, ranging from elephants to lions to camels, and luscious trees run parallel to the road. With perfect weather, the Way and Chang Ling are examples of the most majestic views in Beijing.

Chang Ling

Underground Palace in Ding Ling

Elephants on both sides of Spirit Way

Stone Man on Spirit Way (Shen Lu)

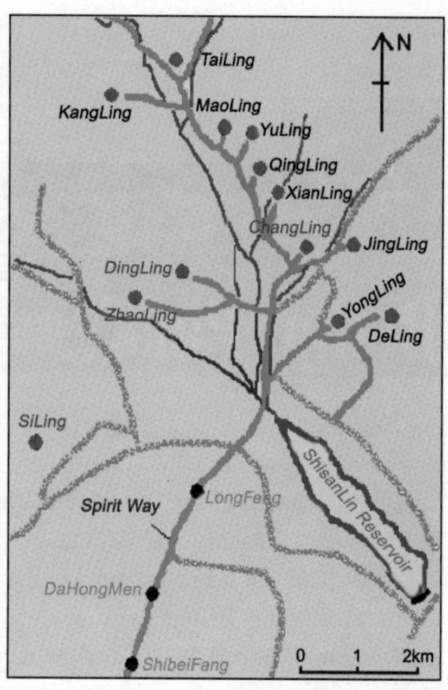

The Thirteen Ming Tombs

Visitor Check List

	Shen Lu	Ding Ling	Chang Ling	Zhao Ling
✉	In a broad valley to the south of Tianshou Mountain			
🚌	Take Bus No.345 to Changping then change to bus No. 314 to Shen Lu, Ding Ling and Chang Ling. Take subway line No.5 or No.13 and exit at Lishuiqiao station. Next, take mini bus No.22 to Shen Lu, Ding Ling and Zhao Ling.			
🕒	8:30-18:00 Daily	8:30-17:30 Daily	8:30-17:30 Daily	8:30-17:30 Daily
☎	86-10-8974-9383	6076-1424	6076-1888	6076-3104
💰	30/20(RMB)	60/40(RMB)	45/30(RMB)	30/20(RMB)
	(Apr.-Oct./Nov.-Mar.)			
⏱	1/2 hour	1 hour	1hour	1 hour

2-7

Beihai Park (北海公园)

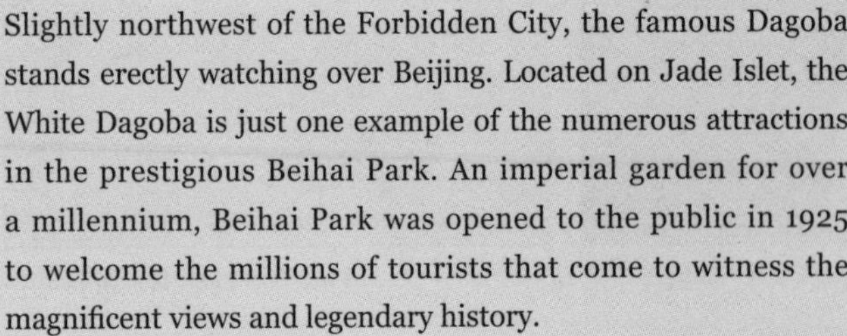

Slightly northwest of the Forbidden City, the famous Dagoba stands erectly watching over Beijing. Located on Jade Islet, the White Dagoba is just one example of the numerous attractions in the prestigious Beihai Park. An imperial garden for over a millennium, Beihai Park was opened to the public in 1925 to welcome the millions of tourists that come to witness the magnificent views and legendary history.

Beihai Park covers an area over 700,000 square meters and is known for its artistic landscaping that is incomparable to anything else. Approximately half of the park flows with gentle water, while the other half, the Jade Islet (Qionghuadao), is where tourists can experience the park's numerous appeals.

The White Dagoba stands 36 meters high on the hills of the island. It's Tibetan-design along with its shining white color which makes a splendid contrast to the unbelievable scenery around the Dagoba. Surrounding the structure, pavilions, man-made hills, hallways, temples, and aesthetic walkways decorate the area. The sacred Dagoba was built in 1651 and stands as an irreplaceable symbol of Beijing.

On the north side of Beihai Park, the Nine-Dragon-Screen is undisputedly the prominent attraction. Stilted 5 meters high, 27 meters long, and 1.2 meters thick, the wall is made of colored, glazed tiles to offer an inspirational experience for tourists.

The White Dagoba

Nine-Dragon Screen

Jade Buddha in Chengguang Dian

The screen was originally put together to fend off evil spirits; ironically, the wall failed to protect anything because the temple that the wall guarded mysteriously vanished.

Jingxinzhai (Heart-Ease Study) is an exquisite garden located on the northern shore of Beihai Lake. All around this garden, the peaceful atmosphere offered a perfect place for emperors to read and study. Jingxinzhai is an elaborate design of a classical Chinese garden.

A Stone Bridge in Jingxinzhai

In the vicinity of the south gate is the Round City (Tuancheng). The Chengguang Dian (hall) is the main structure in Round City. In the hall is a 1.5 meter high statue of Buddha of Sakyamuni, carved out of a very fine, whole piece of white jade. The knife scarred on its left arm was made by the Allied Forces of Eight Powers in 1990.

There is also an expensive but classy restaurant, "The Fangshan" where the Empress Cixi used to dine!

Emperor Qianlong's handwriting of "Qiong dao Chun yin" (Jade Islet Spring Shade) Stele

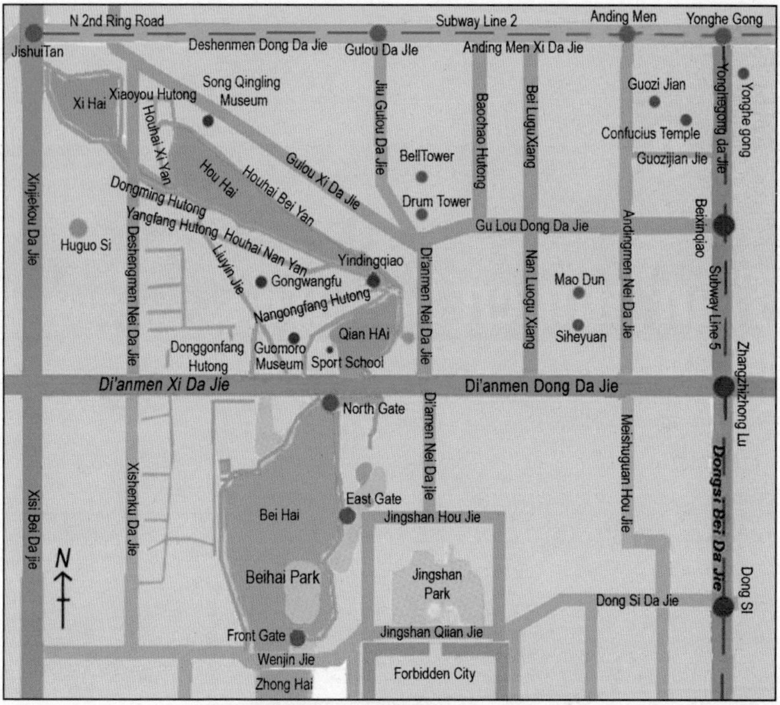

Beihai Park is located in northwest of Forbidden City.

Visitor Check List

✉	1 Wen Jin Lu, Xicheng District, Beijing
🚌	5,13,42,101,103,107,109,111,118,701,812,814,823,846,...
🕒	6:00 am - 8:30 pm (Apr., May., Sep. and Oct.); 6:00 am -10:00 pm (June, July, and Augest); Daily 6:00 am - 8:00 pm (November-March)
☎	86-10-6404-0610 86-10-6403-3225
💰	10 RMB (Winter time is 5 RMB)
⏱	2 hours (Recommended time for a visit time)

2-8 Tian'anmen Square

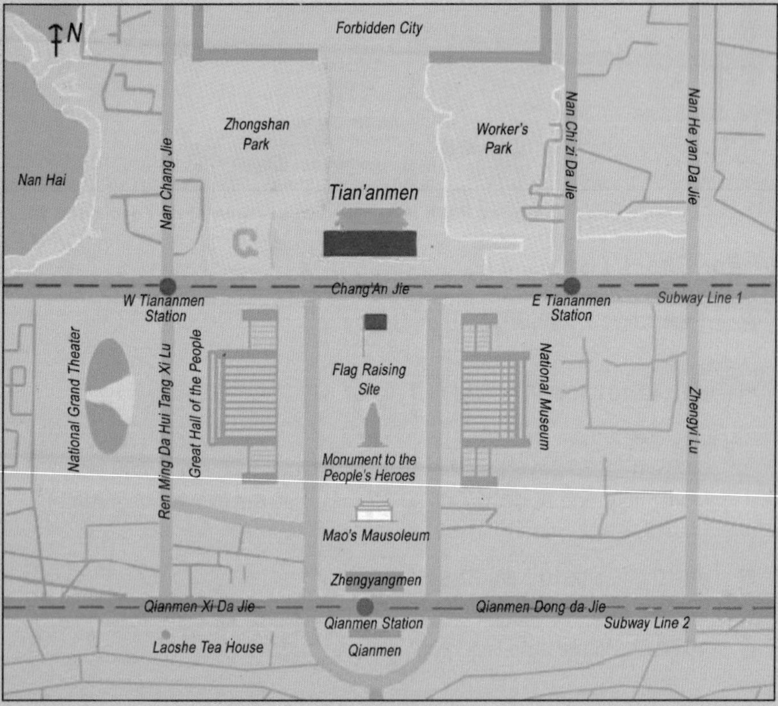

The Map of Tian'anmen Square

Tian'anmen

Located at the very center of Beijing, Tian'anmen was the Forbidden City's gigantic doorway, which is now mostly recognized as the trademark symbol of China (most people instantly identify the picture of Mao Zedong hanging on Tian'anmen). On October 1, 1949, the newly found People's Republic of China held a grand conference here, which ultimately made Beijing the new capital of China. Just as in past times, Tian'an Men Square today holds major events, ceremonies, and public announcements.

Covering over 440,000 square meters, Tian'anmen Square is the largest public square in the world. In fact, it can hold up to one million people at once. Construction of Tian'anmen started in 1417, and it now faces Chang'an Jie, which is one of Beijing's most populous streets. Across the street, hundreds of tourists

The ceiling of Greate Hall of the People

meander around the lively square, and everyday, a flag-raising ceremony takes place at sunrise. Also, a soaring granite obelisk, called the Monument to the People's Heroes, sits at the center of the square to honor the patriots who fought for the New China. Just south of the Monument is Mao Zedong's Mausoleum.

All around the square are museums and halls that reveal China's long history and culture. Some of these include: the

Grate Hall of the People

The seats of the Chinese legislature, the vast auditorium, and banqueting balls are open for part of the day except when the National People's Congress is in session.

Great Hall of the People, China National Museum, and the newly made National Grand Theater. At the very south end of Tian'anmen Square is Qianmen, which was a bastion that once guarded the Forbidden City.

The National Museum of China

Built in 1959, this building was originally home to the Museum of Chinese History and the Museum of the Revolution, which now have merged.

Monument to the People's Heroes and Mao Zedong's Mausoleum

Flag-Raising Ceremony

Zhengyangmen

Jian Lou

Qianmen: Qianmen or Front gate consists of two towers: Zhengyangmen (on the southern edge of Tian'anmen Square) and Jian Lou (just across Qianmen Da jie to the south).

National Grand Theater

2-9 Lugou Bridge

Hurdling 270 meters over the Yongding River, the Lugou Bridge, which is also known as the Marco Polo Bridge, is recognized as one of the most historic landmark of Beijing. In fact, this bridge has survived three major events: Marco Polo's description, Emperor Qianlong's inscription of "Lu Gou Xiao Yue", and the outbreak of the War against the Japan. On July 7, 1937, invading Japanese troops started the comprehensive invasion of China.

Stretched out like a long rainbow, the Lugou Bridge has 11 arches and 140 posts on the sides. On top of the posts, 485 intricately adorned lions sit with lifelike features and poses. The bridge is named as one of the "Eight Scenic Attractions in Yanjing (Beijing)," and it was commemorated

Lugou Bridge

by the famous Italian Marco Polo and Emperor Qianlong for its magnificence.

The Lugou Bridge is located 15 kilometers southwest of Beijing, on the Yongding River beside Wanping Town, Fengtai District. It costs 10 yuan for an adult and 5 yuan for a student to walk across the bridge. To arrive at Lugou Bridge, take bus No.301 or 309, 458, 459, 971 and get off at Diaosuyuan Station (Sculpture Garden). The other way is to take bus No. 310 and get off at Dujiakan Station.

Adorned Lions:

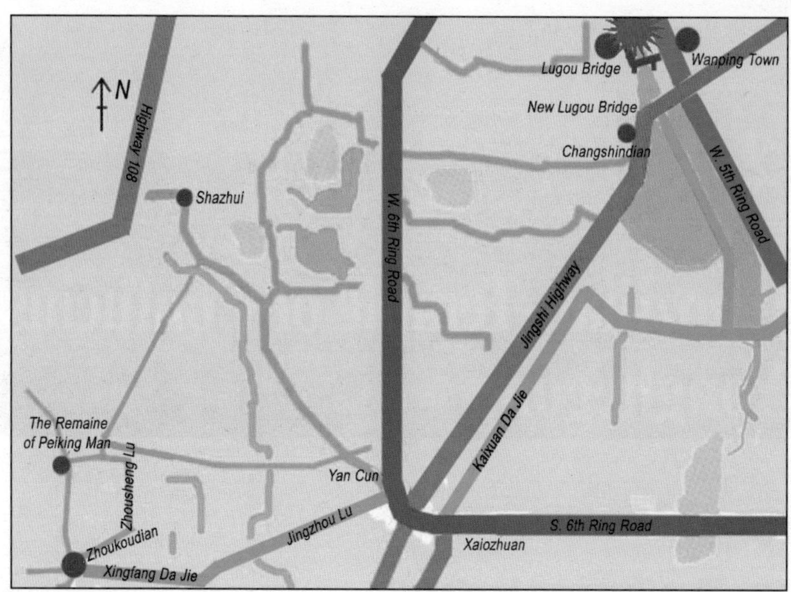

Lugou Bridge is located at the intersection between Jing Shi Highway and West 5th Ring Road

2-10

Guozijian-Temple of Confucius - Yonghegong

Guozijian (Imperial Academy)

Formerly known for its rigorous education, Guozijian, the Imperial Academy, stands today after centuries of history. Just west of the Confucian Temple, the Imperial Academy was constructed in 1306, and later schooled generations of China's highest government officials. Scholars were taught by harsh discipline, and they successfully grew to become intellectual beings educated with the Confucian classics.

Guozijian is in a street called Chengxian Jie

Officials from Yuan, Ming and Qing dynasties all absorbed the prestigious studies offered by the Imperial Academy. At that time, Emperors would visit this academy to pass on knowledge to the students. The

Chengxian Jie

students studied here for three to four years, and after graduation, these graduates were directly set in different levels of government positions. If they could pass the National Imperial Examination, they would obtain the honor of a seat beside the Emperor.

The Imperial Academy remained the system for high level education until it closed in 1905. During that year, new educational systems from the west were adopted and the Chinese culture quickly changed. In that short time frame, the Education Ministry was created and the Imperial Academy's legendary history came to its conclusion.

Visitor Check List

✉	15 Chengxian Jiie. Dongcheng District
🚌	13,18,44,62,104,108,116,807 or Subway at Yonghegong Station. then go south 200 m
🕒	8:30 to 17:00: Daily
☎	86-10-8401-1977
💰	20 RMB (for both Guozijian & Confucius Temple)
⏱	Half to one hour (Recommended time for a visit time)

Temple of Confucius

One of the most famous philosophers in ancient China, even the world, Confucius advocated groundbreaking values and beliefs for family obligations and government. He firmly followed the principles of benevolence and righteousness, and that is why today there are so many temples and halls dedicated to this man. Although he died of unknown causes, Confucius' legacy indefinitely lives on through his Confucianism philosophy.

Today, The Temple of Confucius sits on Guozijian and is the present site of the Capital Museum. Built in 1302, the temple was where emperors of Yuan, Ming and Qing Dynasties worshipped Confucius. The temple is very large, taking up 22,000 square-meters, which is equivalent to 4 courtyards. The area is surrounded with luxuriant trees, and it somewhat resembles a small park. The primary structures of the Temple of Confucius include: Xianshimen (先师门 -gate of Ancient Teacher), Dachengmen (大成门 -Gate of great Accomplishment), Dachengdian (大成殿 -Hall of Great Accomplishment), and Chongshengci (崇圣祠 -Worship Hall).

Confucius Statue

Visitor Check List

✉	13 Chengxian Jie. Dongcheng District
🚌	13,18,44,62,104,108,116,807 or Subway at Yonghegong Station. then go south 200 m
🕒	8:30 to 17:00: Daily
☎	86-10-6407-3593
💰	20 RMB (for both Confucius Temple & Guozijian)
⏱	Half to one hour (Recommended time for a Visit time)

Dachengmen (the Gate of Great Accomplishment)

Yonghegong (Lama Temple)

Located on Yonghegong Da Jie, the Yonghegong, also known as the Lama Temple, is Bejing's largest and most colorful Buddhist temple. It was formerly the imperial residence of Emperor Yongzheng but has been converted into a lamasery temple that is now open to the public. Inside the structure, there are three extravagant archways. Also, there are five central halls, where each hall is designed to be larger than the last, and all halls have courtyards and galleries. Most visitors are fascinated by the 18-meter tall Buddha statue, which was made from a single tree. In addition, keep a lookout for the "Five Hundred Arhats Hill" made of gold, silver, copper, iron and tin, and the niche carved out of certain wood, which gives off a unique fragrance that repels mosquitoes. These three relics are recognized as the "three matchless masterpieces."

The vertical inscribed board with four different languages

Burning incense sticks and making vow to the god

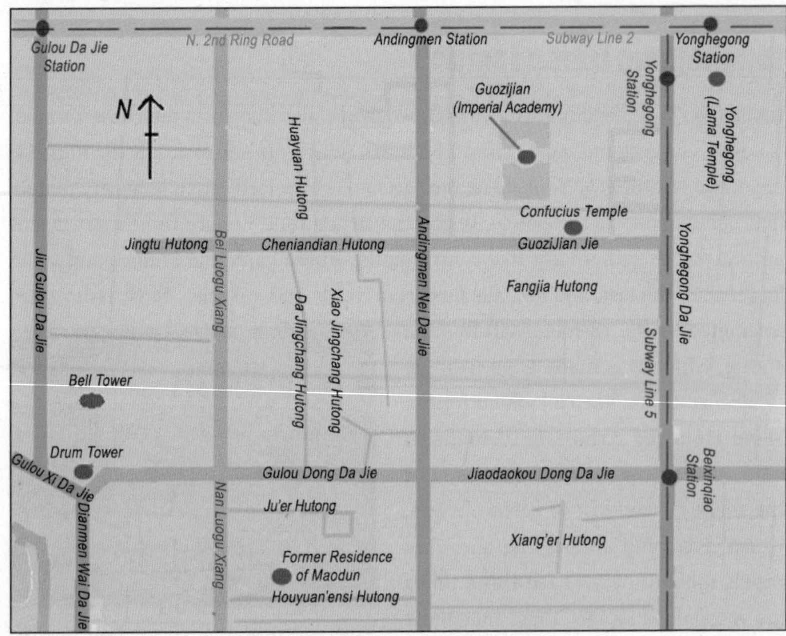

The Map of Guozijian, Confucius Temple and Yonghegong

Scenic Views in Yonghegong

Beautiful Roof

Visitor Check List

✉	12 Yonghegong Da Jie, Dongcheng District
🚌	13,62,116,807 or Subway at Yonghegong Station.
🕘	9:00 to 17:00; Daily
☎	86-10-6404-4499
💰	25 RMB
⏱	Half to one hour (Recommended time for a visit time)

2-11

Best One-day Travel Routes in Beijing

Some of the most dynamic attractions are located in Beijing. The Great Wall, Forbidden City, Ming Tombs, Beijing Hutong... it would take days to fully experience each of these rendezvous. With a jam-packed itinerary, most people need a very short tour of Beijing, while still sampling the Beijing life and culture. Here are some one-day tours that are flexible according to your schedules:

Route One:

Tian'anmen Square - Forbidden City - Jingshan Park -Beihai Park -Shishahai (This route is centered around the downtown area)

Arrive at Tian'anmen Square, the largest public square in the world. Accommodating up to one million people, Tian'anmen Square is 440,00 square meters and the very center of Beijing. You can visit the museums and monuments around the square, including: Great Hall of the People, National Museum, Mao's Mausoleum, and People's Heroes Monument.

Traveling north, you can visit Tian'anmen.

Enter the Gugong or "Forbidden City" from the south entrance Wumen, which is further north of Tian'anmen. Forbidden City is the largest wooden structure in the world, and it was the home of the Emperor and imperial officials during Ming and Qing Dynasties.

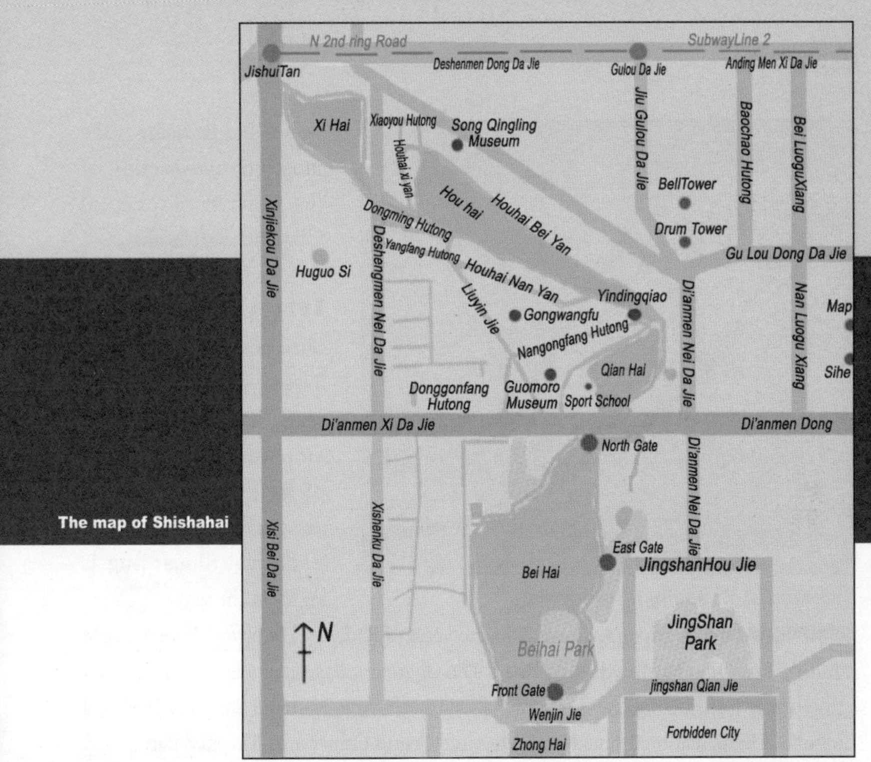

The map of Shishahai

Visit Jingshan Park, which is located north, across the street from the Gugong. From the top of the hill, you can see the entire view of the Gugong. Ming's last Emperor Chongzhen committed suicide here, when Li Zicheng's army entered the city from the south.

Visit Beihai Park, which is just west of Jinshan Park. This is the oldest and best preserved classical imperial garden in the world.

Travel north into the Shishahai area. Complemented with three gorgeous lakes called Qian Hai, Hou Hai, and Xi Hai, Shishahai is filled with gardens, business shops, bars and also leftovers of traditional Beijing residences, Hutongs (alleys) and Siheyuan (a compound with houses around a square courtyard). There are numerous bars and restaurants for you to relax in after a busy day of travel.

Route Two :

Badaling Great Wall - Shisanling (Ming Tombs) – Olympic Green

Travel to Badaling Great Wall. The Great Wall is one of the eight wonders of the

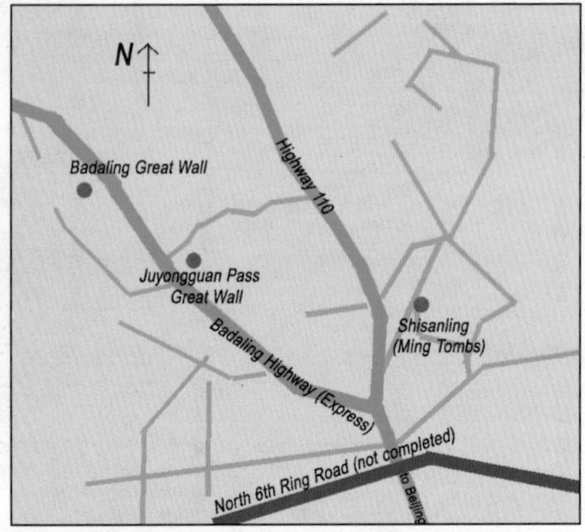

The map of Badaling & Shisanling

world, and Badaling is the most popular section of the Great Wall for local folks and tourists alike.

Turn south east to Shisanling (Ming Tombs). These are the burial grounds of the 13 Ming emperors located north of Beijing City. If you are traveling back from Badaling, Shisanling is right on the way.

Returning to Beijing, Olympic Green is located east of Badaling Highway between north 5th Ring Road and North 4th Ring Road. The Olympic village is in a forest park, and it is the center for the 2008 Summer Bijing Olympic Game. National Stadium, National Indoor Stadium, National Aquatics Center, and Tennis Center are all located here.

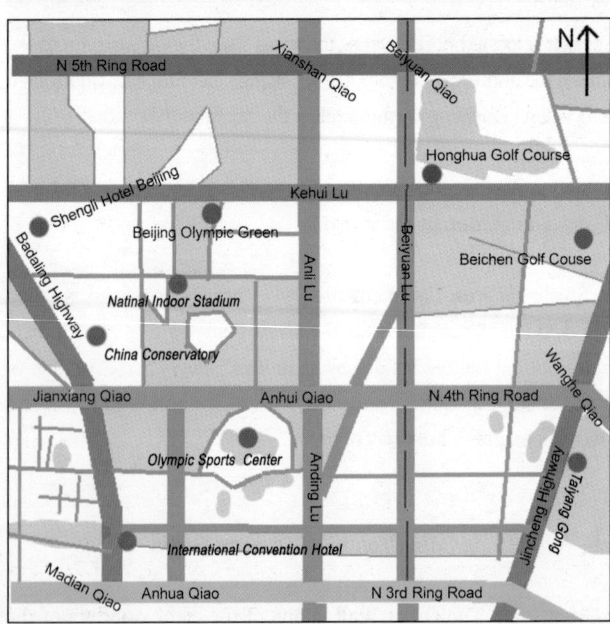

Map of Olympic Green

Route Three:

Forbidden City - Summer Palace – Yuanmingyuan Park - Temple of Heaven

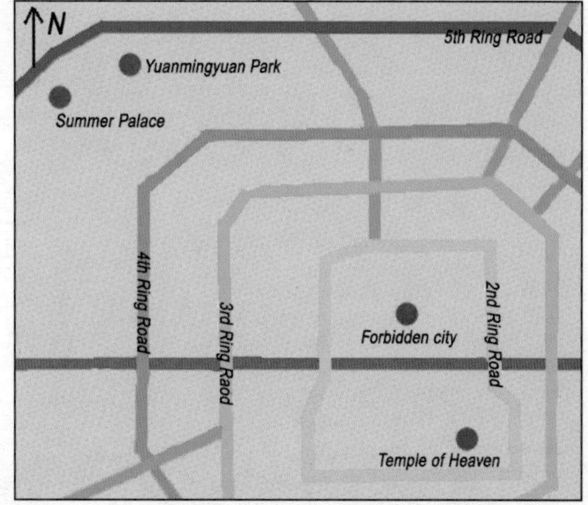

Map of Route Three

This route is one of the most popular options among tourists. It includes Beijing's top attractions: the Forbidden City, Temple of Heaven, Summer Palace, and Yuanmingyuan Park.

Forbidden City - the world's largest wooden palace complex; the former home of the imperial family;

Summer Palace- the imperial garden of Ming and Qing dynasties;

Yuanmingyuan-Located north-east of the Summer palace, it was once the most extolled imperial garden in the world;

Temple of Heaven- the best preserved and largest sacrificial building complex in the world.

Route Four:

To all hikers and nature lovers, the Great Wall Simatai is the place to go. Simatai will undoubtedly leave you with one of the most amazing and unforgettable memories of your life.

Numerous Beijing travel companies offer day tours. Although each may differ with one another, many agencies allow you to pick your own destinations. Having only a short time in China's capital, the flexibility and options of the one-day tours ensure a maximized experience for all tourists. The prices of one-day tours usually range between 40 USD (groups over ten people) to 128 USD (individuals).

Because of China's long history and rich culture, Beijing is the home to over 120 museums. Whether you are interested in architecture, culture, history, celebrities, art, science or nature, Beijing's museums have them all.

For those looking for museum tours, www.tour-beijing.com offers a large collection of Beijing's attractions. Also, you can contact Beijing China trip advisors on this site to customize and create your own tour.

Chapter 3

Museums

3-1 The National Museum of China

The National Museum of China was inaugurated on February 28th, 2003, and is located just east of Tian'anmen Square. A mergence of the National Museum of

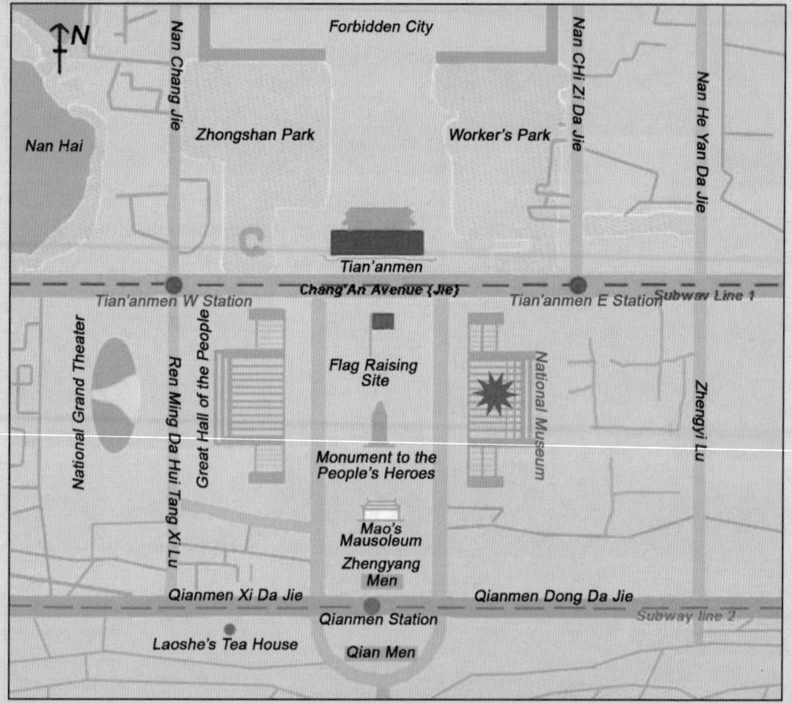

National Museum is located in Tian'anmen Square.

National Museum

Night View of National Museum

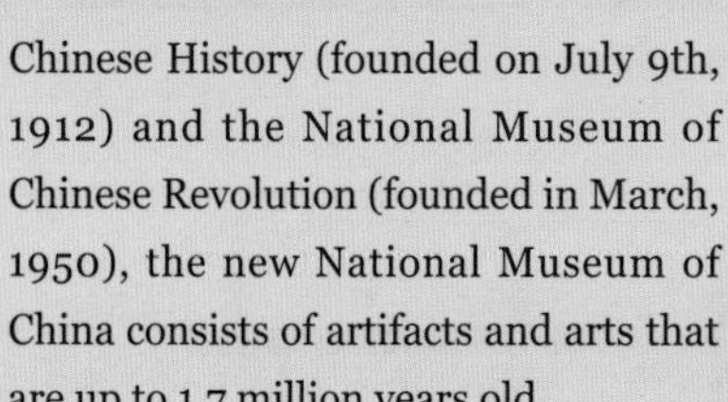

Chinese History (founded on July 9th, 1912) and the National Museum of Chinese Revolution (founded in March, 1950), the new National Museum of China consists of artifacts and arts that are up to 1.7 million years old.

Today, the museum is divided into sections based on time periods; these include the Primitive Society (until 4000 BC), the Slavery Society (2100-475 BC), the Feudal Society (475 BC-1911), the Old Democratic Revolution (1840-1911), the New Democratic Revolution (1911-1949), and the Triumph of the Revolution and the Establishment of Socialism concerning the events since 1949. The National Museum of China is open all 7 days of the week and is closed only on Chinese New Year, so you can be enlightened by its comprehensive display of China's long history and culture anytime.

Visitor Check List

✉	16 East Chang'an Jie, Dongcheng District
🕒	8:30 - 16:30 (Last Entry at 15:00) for Mar.1-Jun.30 8:00 - 18:00 (Last Entry at 17:00) for Jul.1-Aug.31 8:30 - 16:30 (Last Entry at 15:00) for Sep.1-Oct.31 9:00 - 16:00 (Last Entry at 15:00) for Nov.1-Feb.29
☎	86-10-8447-4914
🌐	http://www.nationalmuseum.cn

3-2

National Art Museum of China (Meishuguan)

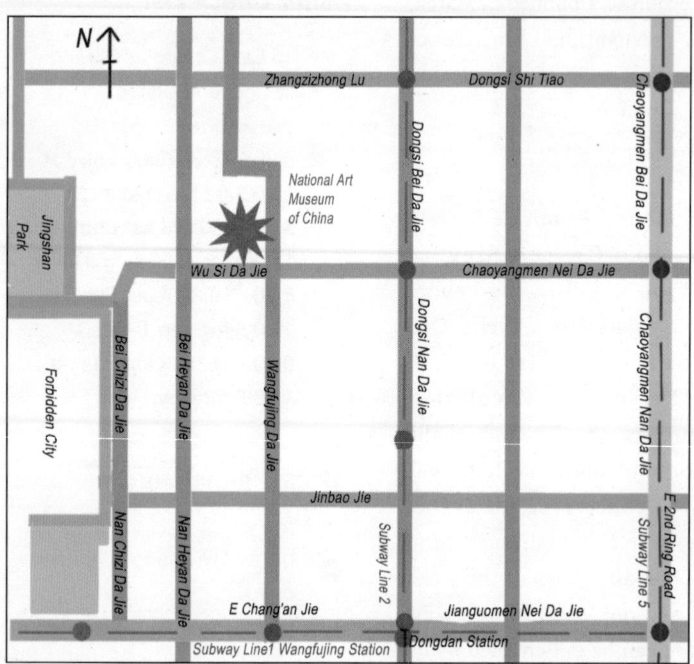

The Map of National Art Museum of China

Meishuguan

National Art Museum of China is one of the country's largest museums dedicated to exhibitions, education, and research of art. Displaying works of artists from an assortment of countries, this museum specializes in modern Chinese paintings, calligraphies, prints and sculptures. Built in the 1950s, this building is styled as a colossal monolith. Today, the National Art Museum of China is becoming increasingly popular for international artists, who frequently hold exhibitions here. There are also art-supply shops nearby that sell books, cards, art supplies, and souvenirs.

Visitor Check List

✉	1 Wusi Da Jie, Dongcheng District
🚌	101, 108, 104, 103, 109, 112, 420, 685, 810, 814, 846 at Meishuguan Station; or Subway line 5 at Dongsi Staion.
🕒	9:00 – 17:00 (Last Entry at 16:00, and opening all year around)
☎	10-6400-6326 / 8403-3500
💰	20 RMB
🌐	www.nationalmuseum.cn

3-3

China National Arts and Crafts Museum

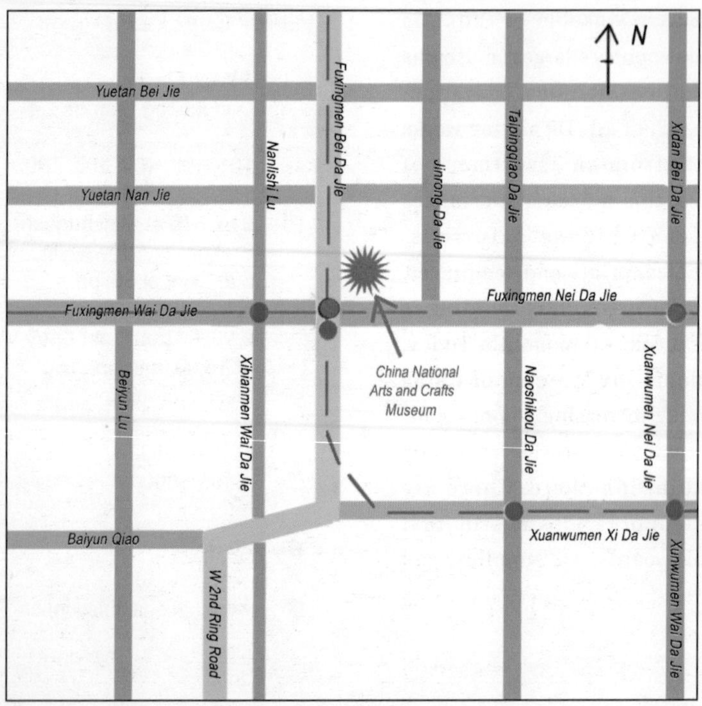

The map of China national Arts and Crafts Museum

China National Arts and Crafts Museum

Located on the fifth floor of Parkson Department Store (Baisheng Shopping Center), China National Arts and Crafts Museum opened in September 1990 and has over 700 displays of contemporary art; you will not find any ancient, dusty artifacts here. Instead, there is a very interesting collection of modern works, ranging from oddly carved lumps of jade to strangely posed monuments. However, this museum satisfactorily portrays the works of modern artists and illustrates the evolving tastes in art and their origins. Epitomizing exhibits include clay figurines from Jiangsu, cloisonné from Beijing, lacquer ware from Fujian, and ceramics from Jingdezhen Town. These examples attract great attention and shine light upon China's artistic values.

Visitor Check List

✉	101 Fuxingmen nei Da Jie, Xicheng District
🚌	Subway Line 1 or Bus:1, 4, 10, 15, 52, 57, 802 at Fuxingmen Station.
🕘	9:30 – 16:00, Teusday - Sunday
☎	86-10-6605-3476
💰	4 RMB

3-4

Memorial Museum of Chinese People's Anti-Japanese War

Displaying almost 900 exhibits, the Memorial Museum of Chinese People's Anti-Japanese War is located in Wanping Town, which is right next to the famous Marco Polo Bridge – also known as the Lugou bridge. This museum houses 3800 photos and portraits, and 5000 cultural artifacts. The comprehensive halls display the whole sequence of Anti-Japanese War and include the recovered scenes of historic events,

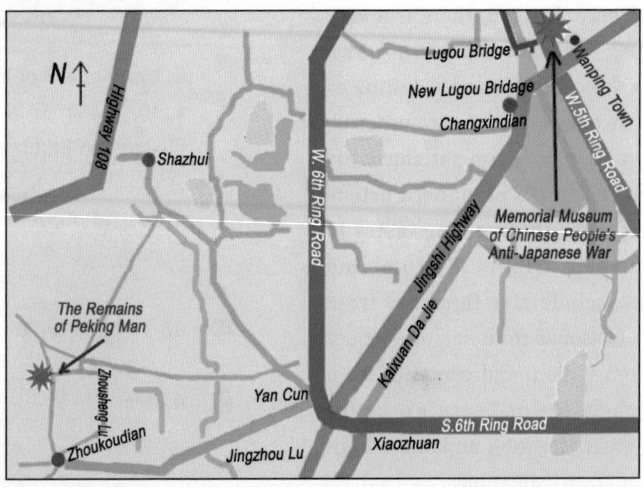

Map of Memorial Museum of Chinese People's Anti-Japanese War

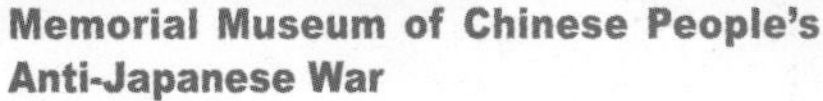

Memorial Museum of Chinese People's Anti-Japanese War

1 Wanping Town
2 Marco Polo Bridge – also known as the Luguo Qiao

such as the Nanjing Massacre. This museum has many enlightening exhibits, including the Prelude of the Anti-Japanese War, Strategic Defense of the War, Strategic Confrontations, Chinese War Zone of After the Breakout of the Pacific War, and Final Victory of the Anti-Japanese War.

The Lugou Bridge is Beijing's oldest bridge, and it lies across the Yongding River. Today, the Lugou Bridge is commemorated as the spot where invading Japanese armies fiercely clashed with Chinese soldiers on July 7, 1937, which commenced Japan's 8-year occupation in China. Because of its historic appropriateness and relationship, many connect the museum to this bridge.

The Memorial Museum of Chinese People's Anti-Japanese War houses some of the most up-to-date exhibitions. Ranging from video-audio technologies to battlefield simulations, this museum ensures an entertaining and enlightening experience.

Visitor Check List

	101 Nei Jie, Wanping Town, Fengtai District, Beijing
	Bus 301, 309, 458, 459,937 (branch), at Diaosuyuan Station.
	8:00-16:30 (16:00 stop selling tickets)
	86-10-8389-3136
	15 RMB; 8 RMB for college students; Free for others.

3-5

The Remains of Peking Man in Zhoukoudian

Over 500,000 years ago, on the footsteps of Dragon Bone Mountain, the Peking Man roamed freely. In 1927, Chinese archeologists discovered the ancient remains of the Peking Man and designated them as the fossils of one of the most primitive kind of homo-sapiens. After the discovery of the first complete Homo erectus skull cap, archeologists appointed the finding of the Peking Man as the paramount discovery for

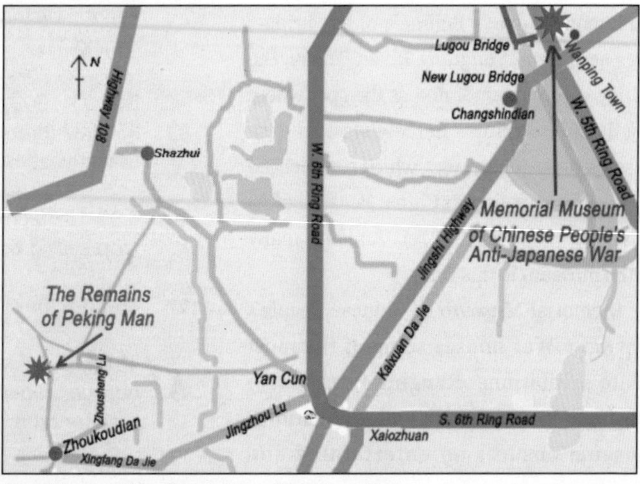

The Map of The Remains of Peking Man

The Remains of Peking Man

The Place that found the fossils

studies of mankind's evolution.

Following the breakthrough of the Peking Man, many others followed. Numerous tools were uncovered along with teeth and evidences of fire. More importantly to the scientific research, more and more pieces of the skeleton were unearthed. Unfortunately during the War of Resistance Against Japanese Aggression, these vital pieces were mysteriously lost. Despite the loss, the UNESCO listed the Peking Man site as one of the world's heritages in 1987.

Today, there is a museum to showcase some of the Neanderthal lifestyle. There are exhibits of tools and statues of Peking Man and other ape-men found all around China. Also, tourists can follow the trails to explore the excavation site.

Visitor Check List

✉	1 Zhoukoudian Da Jie, Fangshan District
🚌	Take Bus No. 917 at Tianqiao bus terminus, or take bus No. 616 at Beijing West Railway Staion, then change to a special-line bus at Liangxiang or Fangshan. to Zhoukoudian. To drive a car, get onto the Beijing-Shijiazhuang Expressway and get out at the exit of Yancun, then turn right at Zhoukoudian.
🕒	8:30 – 17:00
☎	86-10-6930-1287
💰	30 RMB/Adult, 15 RMB/ Student & Senior

Hutong and Siheyuan make up the majority of old Beijing. Siheyuan is a type of housing found all throughout Beijing, and in fact, it literally translates to "a courtyard with four surrounding buildings." However, the lack of private toilets and squalid living conditions make these Siheyuan complexes less and less popular. Hutongs are the narrow alleys formed between rows of Siheyuan buildings, and people mostly walk or ride bikes down these pathways. In old China, people distinguished 36-meter-wide roads as big streets and an 18-meter-wide road as a small street. However, a 9-meter-wide lane was always called a Hutong. Some of these are only 10 meters long and 40 centimeters wide, while others can have over 20 different turns. Since the Yuan Dynasty (1206-1368), the combination of Hutong and

Hutong

The door of a Siheyuan

Chapter 4

Hutong & Siheyuan

This Siheyuan was one of Li Lianying's many houses. Li Lianying was a royal eunuch during the Qing Dynasty, and was the favorite of Empress Dowager Cixi. He served as the Head Eunuch (太监总管) until 1908, where he had overriding dominance in many important court affairs and other official decisions. Making fortunes out of bribery, Li Lianying lived in this Siheyuan for a period of time.

Siheyuan was the primary layout all around Beijing until around 1950. Interestingly, wealthier class people use to occupy these communities, where larger sized Siheyuan symbolized more wealth. Hutongs and Siheyans are rich in culture, showing the Beijing folk life at its realist. Today, demolitions are taking place in order to create more room for cozy apartment complexes and businesses. Despite the loss, these complexes are still an important part to Beijing's history and culture. A stroll around the Forbidden City will lead you into a maze of Hutongs and Siheyuans.

The West Route of Hutong Tour

The West Route is focused on the Shishahai area.

Located northwest of the Forbidden City, the Shishahai area is a popular Hutong tour site among tourists today. The region is complemented with three gorgeous lakes called Qianhai (meaning "Front Sea"), Houhai (meaning "Back Sea"), and Xihai (meaning "Western Sea"). All around the Shishahai area, there are scenic views of the lakeside. Having a history dating back to the Jin Dynasty, this beautiful region is also filled with leftovers of traditional Beijing residences, Hutongs and Siheyuans. It is often said that Shichahai is one of Beijing's best places to witness well-preserved Hutong and Siheyuan.

1. Start at the corner of Di'anmen Xi Da Jie and Qianhai Xi Jie. Then go north; Guo Moruo's former residence is located on this street. Guo Moruo (1892-1978) was one of China's most gifted writers.

On your right side you can see a famous athletics school. Jet Li was graduated from this school.

2. Go East to Hehua Market . This is a bar area (before was Antique Market) beside the lake of Qianhai.

3. Go North on Qianhai Bei Yan to Yinding Bridge (Silver Ingot Bridge). Yinding Bridge is a white marble bridge, which represents a centuries-old landmark that separates Houhai and Qianhai. Rowboats frequently float past under this bridge as the oarsmen appreciate the romantic clash between

1 Qianhai
2 Hehua Market
3 Guo Moruo's Former Residence

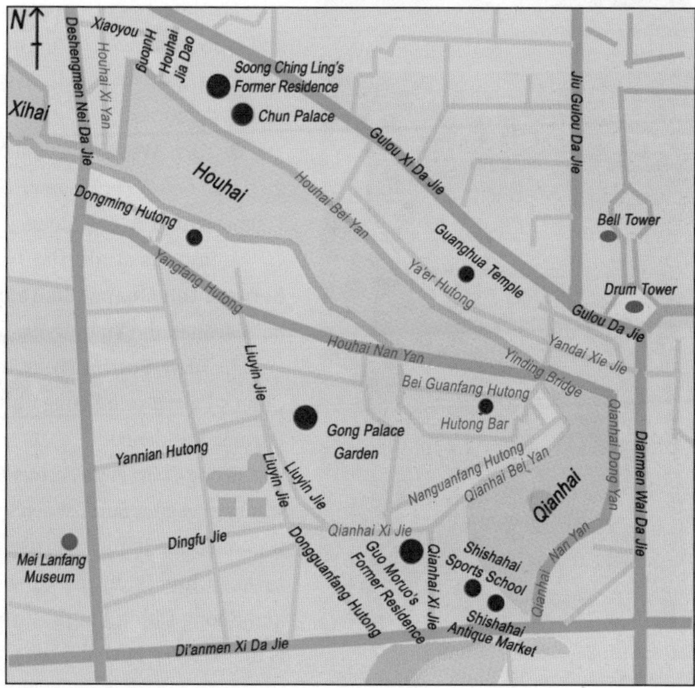

The Map of Shishahai Area

Yinding Qiao

Address: 38 Yandai Xie Jie Named "Meiren Ji" Sells traditional Chinese clothes

civilization and nature all around. A famous BBQ restaurant "Kaorouji" is just in front of the Bridge.

4. Cross the bridge and turn east on Yandai Xie Jie. Yandai means tobacco pipe, and xie jie means diagonal street.

5. Continue East to Di'anmen Wai Da Jie then turn North to Drum Tower and Bell Tower.

Constructed in 1420, the Drum Tower has one large drum accompanied by 24 smaller drums. This tower was used to signal every hour of the day. Today, visitors can climb the drum tower to watch over the city and inspect the intricate drums.

The Bell Tower was made in 1745 and is located near the Drum Tower. There is a 42-ton bell suspending within the tower.

6. Turn West on Gulou Xi Da Jie then turn onto Ya'er Hutong. Guanghua Temple is at 31 Ya'er Hutong.

A famous Buddhist temple in Beijing, the Guanghua Temple was built around the Yuan Dynasty.

7. Turn South-West to Prince Chun's Palace and Soong Ching Ling's Former Residence.

Soong Ching ling's Former Residence was named after Sun Yat-sen's wife, and was once the living quarters for both Prince Chun from the Qing Dynasty and Soong Ching Ling's. Prince Chun is the father of Puyi, the last emperor of China. Prince Chun frequently enjoyed

1 Yandai Xie Jie
2 Bell Tower
3 The Big Bell
4 Drums
5 Drum Tower

the picturesque gardens here, and today, many of Soong Ching Ling's old photos and letters are on display.

8. Go West on Xiaoyou Hutong. The renowned Jiumen Xiao Chi is in this Hutong. There are a lot of traditional Beijing snacks for sale here.

9. Go South on Houhai Xi Yan and Dongming Hutong. Next, go south east on Yangfang Hutong and South on Liuyin Jie to Prince Gong' Palace Garden.

Built in 1777, Prince Gong's Palace Garden used to be the home of He Shen, a notorious, unlawful minister under Emperor Qianlong. He Shen used the country's money to build this luxurious palace, which ultimately led to his execution. He Shen's palace later

6 Guanghua temple
7 Soong Ching Ling's Former Residence

Prince Gong's Palace has very pictureque gardens.

became the home of Prince Gong, the brother of Emperor Xiangfeng. Today, it has a beautiful garden and is open for the public to enjoy.

10. Alternative Route: You can go south on Deshengmen Wai Da Jie, turn right on Huguosi Jie. Mei Lanfang Museum is at 9 Huguosi Jie. (Tel: 86-10-6618-3598, 9:00-16:00, 6 RMB)

11. Go back to Qianhai Xi Jie

"Gong Wang Fu" (Prince Gong's Palace)
This is inscribed on this tablet in Fu Jie's hand writing (Fu Jie is last Emperor Fu Yi's Brother)

Mei Lanfang Memorial Museum

Mei Lanfang (1894-1961) is one of China's most famous opera masters, and represents a symbol of China's performing arts.

Exhibits in the Museum

4-2

The East Route of Hutong Tour

The East Route is focused on the North East Forbidden City Area

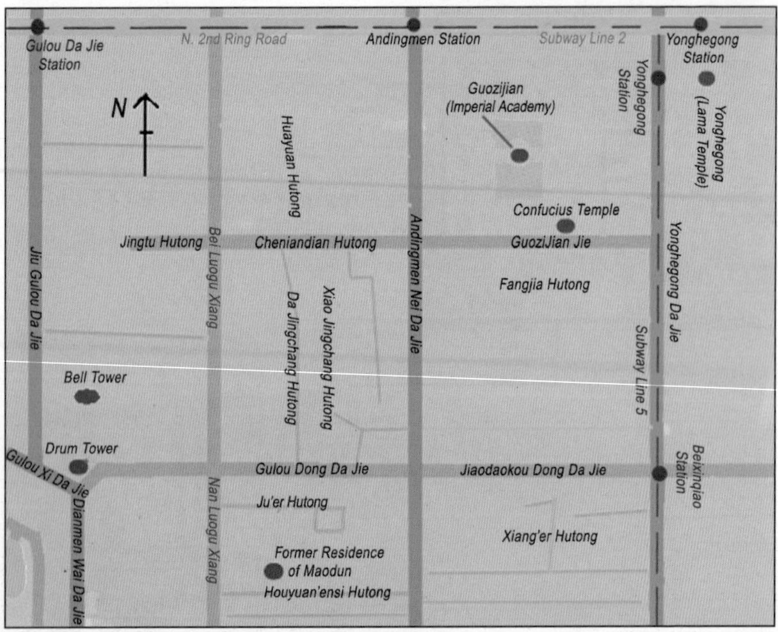

The map of the Area of East of Gulou Da Jie

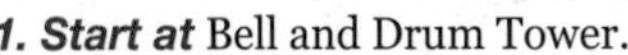

1. Start at Bell and Drum Tower.

2. Go East on Gulou Dong Da Jie then turn south on Nan Luoguxiang.

Nan Luoguxiang is a famous street at the old heart of Beijing. The street is lined with hole-in-the-wall cafes, restaurants, music shops, bookstores, massage boutiques, vintage clothing shops, smoothie joints, street food and bars.

3. Turn East at No. 13 of Hou Yuan'en Si. This is Mao Dun's former residence. Author of many short stories and famous works, such as Midnight and Spring Silkworms, Mao Dun (real name is Shen

1 The Drum Tower
2 The Street Signs
3 Nan Luoguxiang Street
4 "Xiaoxin Café" at 103 Nan Luoguxiang
5 "Pass by Bar" at 108 Nan Luoguxiang
6 HongrenFang Cafe at 111 Nan Luoguxiang
7 Nan Luoguxiang Street

Former Residence of Mao Dun

Guozijian Jie (Street)

On the tour

Dehong) was a novelist, critic, journalist, and even the Chinese Minister of Culture at one point of his lifetime. Today, he is one of the most recognized Chinese novelists.

4. Go North on Andingmen Nei Da Jie, then turn East on Guozijiian Jie. You will see Guozijian is at No.15 Guozijiian Jie. Next, the Temple of Confucius is at No.13 Guozijiian Jie.

Guozijian – Constructed in 1306, Guozijian was an Imperial Academy, where the highest government officials were educated. It was closed in 1905 after new educational systems from the west were introduced. (Details see Chapter 2)

Confucius – Accredited as ancient China's greatest thinker and philosopher, Confucius (551-479BC) introduced the Confucian theory, which continues to be an important element of traditional Chinese culture. (Details see Chapter 2)

5. After visiting Guozijian and Confucius Temple, keep going on east then turn north on Yonghegong Da Jie. Soon, you will arrive at the famous Lama Temple "Yonghegong". The largest and best preserved temple in Beijing, Lama Temple "Yonghegong" is one of the most well-known and colorful temples in Beijing. (Details see Chapter 2).

※ There are some local Traveling Companies offering the tour of Hutong. Beijing Hutong Tour Co., LTD is a good tour agency. Please check the website: http://www.hutongtour.com.cn

※ Also, there are many locals who are more than willing to give you a ride and a tour of the Hutong.

Chapter 5

Dining in Beijing

Beijing's culinary experience is just as varied as the cultural experiences in China's capital. From noodles to dumplings to hot pots, Beijing has a flavor for everyone's picky tastes. Each restaurant offers its unique sauces and flavoring specialties. Of course, restaurants are not restricted to Chinese cuisines; you can expect to find assorted restaurants offering foods from other nations as well. Whether you like Italian, French, Chinese, or even fast food, you can be certain that you can satisfy your hunger in Beijing.

5-1

Beijing Roast Duck

A trip to Beijing is essentially pointless without sampling China's prized Beijing Roast Duck. Missing this experience is like missing the Great Wall!

First served during the Yuan Dynasty, the Beijing Roast Duck has survived the test of time; actually, the test of taste. Ducks are specially raised for this dish, and after 65 days, these ducks are slaughtered and seasoned before they are roasted in unique ovens. The Beijing Roast Duck is a mouth-watering, smoked meal accompanied by pancakes, sauce, vegetable fillings and savoring pieces of crispy skin that lusciously melt in your mouth.

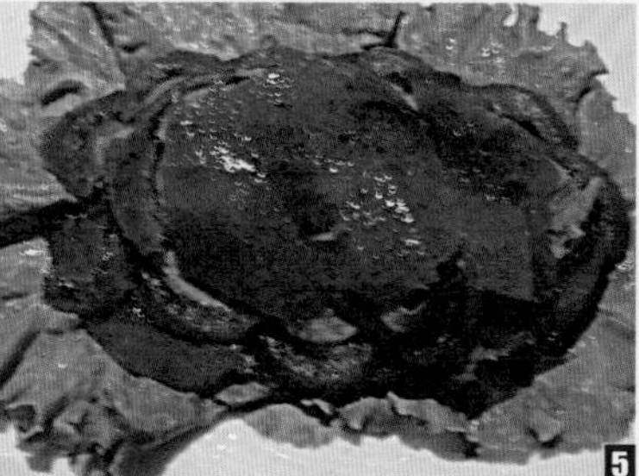

1 Roasting Ducks
2 Slitting Roasted Duck
3 Warm and soft crepes (pancakes)
4 Condiment
5 A Dish of cut crispy roasted crust
6 Spread the condiment on the crepe, add sugar and/or garlic as you may wish, then put the duck in the middle of the crepe and add greens you preferred. Roll and eat your own duck roll

Quanjude

Quanjude is one of Beijing's most renowned restaurants, most often complimented for its trademark Quanjude Roast Duck. Since 1864, Quanjude has left a 140 year old culinary legacy, making it a vital stop on your trip in Beijing. Today, Quanjude has already served over 115 million ducks. To obtain the unique flavor of its roast duck, chefs use half-opened ovens called Gualu to bake the duck. With crispy skins and savory aromas, Quanjude Roast Duck offers one of Beijing's finest culinary experience.

Quanjude Qianmen Restaurant

The Information about some Quanjude Roast Duck Restaurants:

1. Quanjude Roast Duck Qianmen Restaurant

Address	32 Qianmen Da Jie, Chongwen District
Tel	86-10-67011379
Bus	110,819,59 at Dashila Station or 20, 17, 53, 22 at Qianmen Station
Parking	Unavailable
Price	Approx 150 RMB per Person
Card	Usable

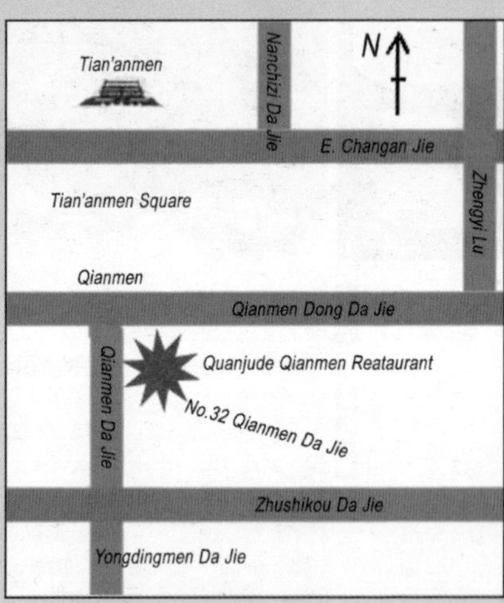

2. Quanjude Peking Roast Duck Hepingmen Restaurant

Address	14 Qianmen Xi Da Jie, Chongwen District
Tel	86-10-63018833
Bus	14, 7, 15 or Subway Line 2 at Qianmen Station
Parking	Available
Price	Approx 150 RMB per Person
Card	Usable

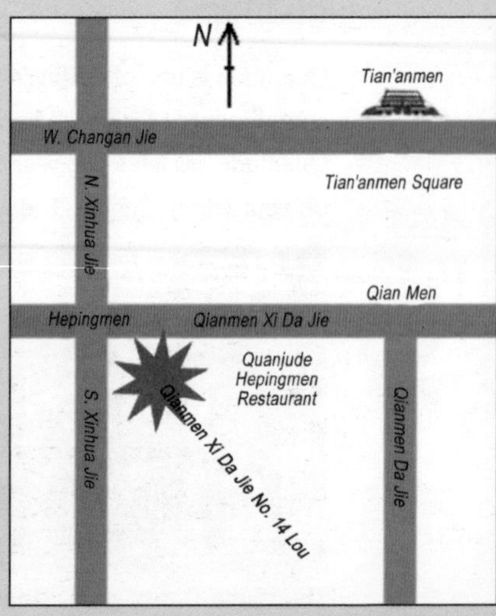

3. Quanjude Roast Duck Wangfujing Restaurant

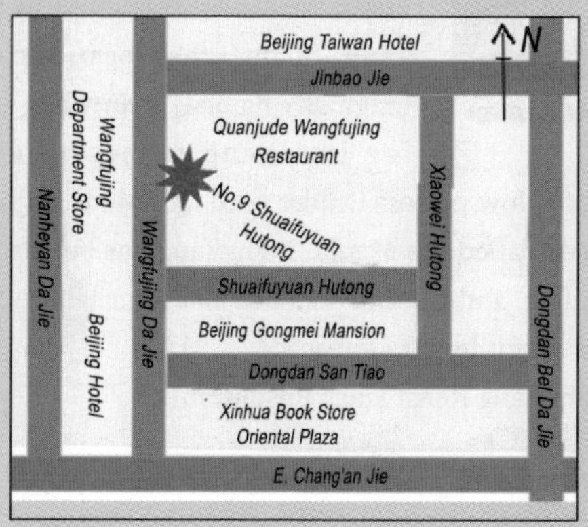

✉	9 Shuaifuyuan Hutong, Wangfujing Da Jie, Dongcheng District
☎	86-10-65253310
🚌	1,3,4,8,10,20,37,52, 103,104,110,106,108, 802,803,807 and subway at Wangfujing Station
P	Unavailable
$	Approx.150 RMB per Person
Card	Usable

4. Quanjude Roast Duck Yayuncun Restaurant

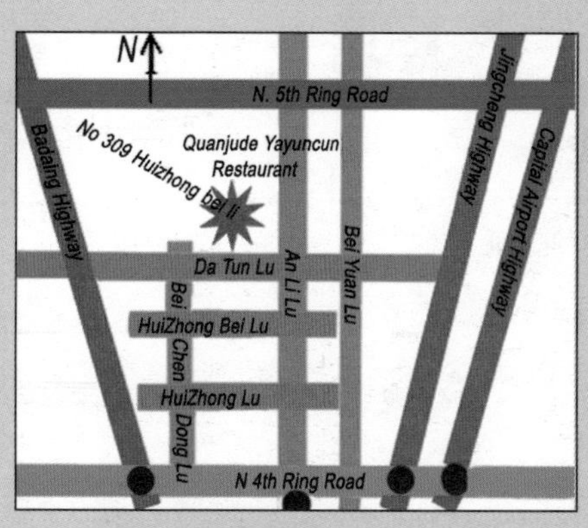

✉	309 Huizhongbeili, A. Chaoyang District
☎	86-10-64801686
🚌	108, 941, 985, 803 at Huizhongbeili Station
P	Available
$	Approx 150 RMB per Person
Card	Usable

Bianyifang

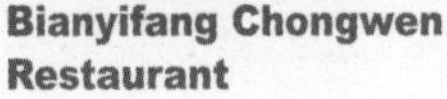
Bianyifang Chongwen Restaurant

Bianyifang Hademen Restaurant

With over 100 years of history, Bianyifang has the longest history among the major restaurants in Beijing and in many other locations. Originally named "Pianyifang" for its cheap prices, the restaurant still sells delicious ducks at low prices. Unlike both Quanjude and Da Dong, chefs here use a unique oven called the Menlu. Bianyifang has been a culinary escape for numerous years now, and the convenience and affordability makes this place an attractive restaurant for hungry tourists.

The Information about some Bianyifang Roast Duck Restaurants:

1. Bianyifang Chongwen Restaurant

	A 2 Chongwenmen Wai Da Jie, Chongwen District
	86-10-67120505
	39, 43, 807, 803 at Huashi Station
	Available (5 RMB/hour)
	Approx. 150 RMB per Person
	Accepted

2. Bianyifang Xingfu Restaurant

	36 Xingfu Da Jie,Chongwen District
	86-10-67116545
	8, 41, 822, 957, 958 at Xingfu Da Jie Station
	Available
	Approx 100 RMB per Person
	Accepted

Da Dong

Da Dong Tuanjiehu Restaurant

Today, Da Dong is one of Beijing's most popular restaurants among locals and tourists alike. Da Dong is the capital's newest major culinary attraction, and is unsurprisingly booked all the time. The menus come in English and have pictures to help, so language barriers will not interfere with your appetite. Just like Quanjude, Da Dong uses the half-opened ovens – known as the gualu – to roast its ducks. However, Da Dong is especially recognized for its low-fat food; unlike the greasy ducks offered in most other restaurants, Da Dong chefs promotes good taste as well as good health. This restaurant also provides a large variety of dipping sauces, ensuring that every customer's unique taste is satisfied.

The Information about Da Dong Roast Duck Restaurant:

1. Da Dong Tuanjiehu Restaurant:

✉	Tower #3 Tuanjiehu Bei Kou, Chaoyang District
☎	86-10-6582-2892
Bus	705, 943 and Yuntong 117, 113 at Baijiazhuang Station.
P	Available
$	Approx 200 RMB per Person
Card	Accepted

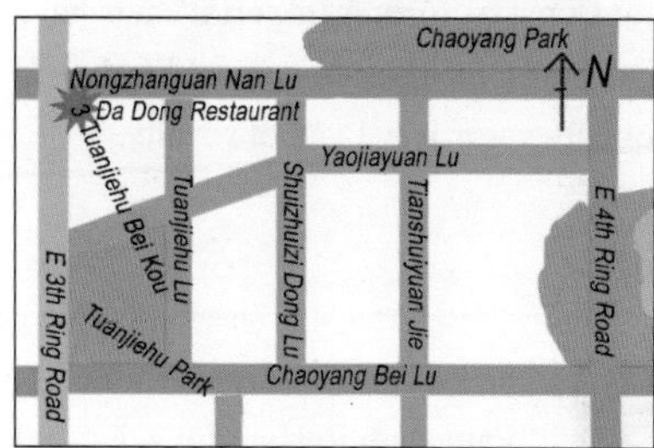

2. Da dong Dongsi restaurant:

✉	A 22 Dong Si Shi Tiao, Dongcheng District
☎	86-10-5169-0328
Bus	113, 115, 118 at West Dongsidshitiao, or subway at Dongsishitiao
P	Available (5 RMB/4 hours)
$	Approx 200 RMB per Person
Card	Accepted

5-2

Royal Cuisine

During the Qing Dynasty, emperors and their families feasted on delicious foods called the Royal Cuisine, which was cooked by the imperial kitchen. The chefs paid astute attention to each dish's taste and also made certain that the plate retained an aesthetic value as well. The food actually originated among Han and Manchu people, but after the fall of the Qing Dynasty, former imperial chefs have opened Royal Cuisine restaurants all around China for the pleasure of locals and tourists. Today, anyone can sample the exquisite yet pricey taste of royalty.

Fangshan

First opened in 1925, Fangshan Restaurant is located in Beihai Park and is another fine example of Beijing's Royal Cuisine experiences. This restaurant was originally owned by former Qing Dynasty imperial chefs, and at that time, Fangshan was one of the best restaurants in Beijing.

Serving high-priced dishes today, Fangshan is, however, not recognized for its

actual food but for its grandeur environment. The restaurant is situated in a traditional courtyard and faces the relaxing lake. In fact, Fangshan sits directly in a section of the Beihai palace, where lovely dancers greet you in the courtyard.

The further information of Fangshan Restaurant:

1 Fangshan is located in Beihai Park.
2 The Beautiful Ceiling of Fangshan Fanzhuang
3 Replica of Emperor's Chair in the Fangshan Fanzhuang
4 Everything is in China's Royal Color: The Yellow Chinese word "Shou," meaning long life, is on every dish.

✉	1 Wenjin Jie (inside Beihai Park), Xicheng District
☎	86-10-64011889
🚌	5, 13, 101, 103, 109, 810 at Beihai Station.
P	Available
$	Approx. 150 RMB per Person
💳	Accepted

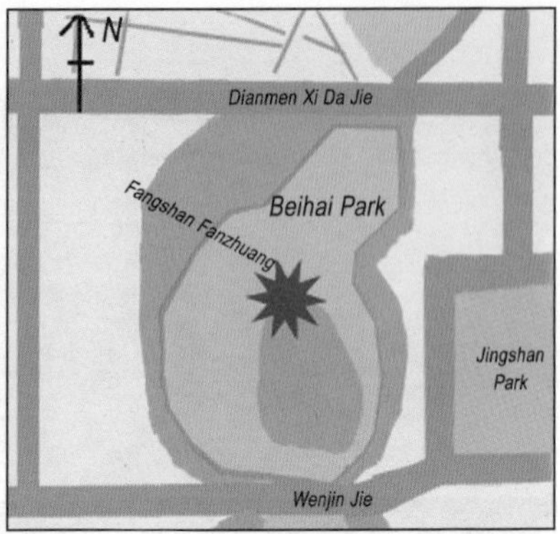

Lijiacai (The Legend of Family Li Cuisine)

In 1985, the Li family established Lijiacai, which quickly became one of the most renowned restaurants in Beijing. The restaurant chefs use a secret recipe passed down from an ancestor of the Li family, who worked in the imperial kitchen during the Qing Dynasty. The actual restaurant is located in a ridged, old house, but this is one case when it's the inside that counts. US presidents and corporate leaders have all dined here before. The

Lijiacai Restaurant is located in old Hutong.

Restaurant is not fancy, but the food is extremely tasty.

food here is pricey, but customers say the food is worth every cent. Unlike normal restaurants, Lijiacai does not have a menu; you simply tell the waiter how much you want to spend, and the chef will supply a banquet. The restaurant is very small and has only a few tables, so unless you want to be hungry, make a reservation at least two days before.

The further information of Lijiacai Restaurant:

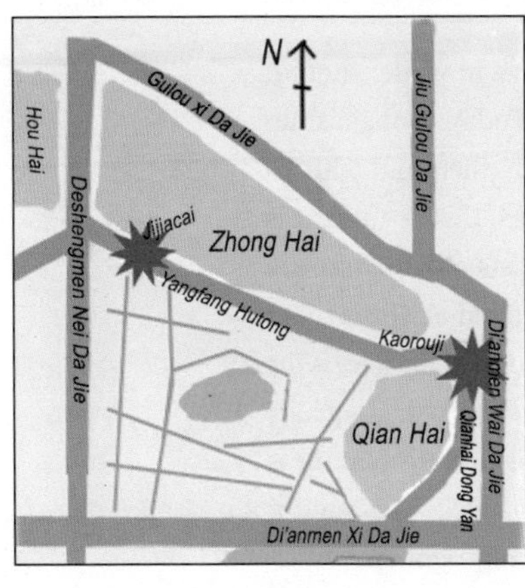

✉	11 Yangfang Hutong, Deshengmen Nei Da Jie, Xicheng District
☎	86-10-6618-1017
🚌	55 at Deshengmen Station
P	Available
$	Approx 300 RMB per Person
💳	Accepted

5-3

Beijing and Regional Cuisine

Besides the sizzling Beijing Roast Duck and the majestic Royal Cuisine, Beijing is a culinary focal point for countless other styles of food. The chows come from all geographic divisions of Chinese cuisine, varying from Sichuan style to Mongolian style. Interestingly, the menu-favorites depend on season – for example, hotpot is the number one choice during winter. Whether you are looking for a full meal of mutton or a nibble at some traditional Beijing snacks, the streets of Beijing have them all.

Donglaishun

When the bitingly cold temperatures arrive in winter, hotpot composes the majority of Beijing's diet. Today, Donglaishun Restaurant is the city's primary hotpot supplier, and with its respected history of over one hundred years, this restaurant is extremely popular among locals and tourists alike. There are hundreds of Donglaishun Restaurant scattered all throughout China, and many are centered in Beijing. The specialty here is the mutton dish. Renowned for the paper-thin slices of high-quality meat and excellent dipping sauce, Donglaishun Restaurant is opened for lunch and dinner seven days a week. The mouth-watering dishes here will definitely fill your belly right up.

Donglaishun Beijing HualongJie Branch

The Hotpot Table of Donglaishun Restaurant

List of Some Donglaishun Restaurants in Beijing Area

Beijing Branch Name	Branch Address	Phone No.
Xin Dong'an	130 Wangfujing Da Jie, Dongcheng District	10-65280932
Wangfujing	198 Wangfujing Da Jie, Dongcheng District	10-65139661
Hualong Jie	E Hualong Jie, Nanheyan Da Jie, Dongcheng District	10-65595084
Baojing	189 Andingmen Wai Da Jie, Dongcheng District	10-64401116
Haidian	25 Yiheyuan Lu, Haidian District	10-62875962
Xisanqi	2 Yuxinghuayuan, Haidian District	10-82957740
Shazikou	71 Lelin Lu, Chongwen District	10-67210328
Liangxiang	12 Liangxiangxilu Nan Da Jie, Fangshan District	10-69373766
Tian'anmen	44 Dongjiaominxiang, Dongcheng District	10-65241042
Kuishenxing	15 Xiaoyun Lu, Chaoyang District	10-64601084
Chengxiang	A 23 5-5 Fuxing Lu 5-5, Haidian District	10-68296775
Panjiayuan	31 Huaweibeili, Chaoyang District	10-67781952
Zhongzhoulu	Building 3 North Liupukang, Dongcheng District	10-62379230
Dengshikou	141 Wangfujing Da Jie, Dongcheng District	10-65279188
Wanshoulu	B 63 Fuxing Lu, Haidian District	10-68223263
Jianguomen	2 Xiaoyangmao Hutong, Jiannei, Dongcheng District	10-65241387
Haoyuan	19 Jiannei Da jie (Haoyuan Hotel), Dongcheng District	10-65286140
Fengtai	90 Fengtai Lu, Fengtai District	10-63811934
Xinjiekou	99 Xinjiekou Bei Da Jie, Xicheng District	10-82211079
Xidan	23 Lingjing Hutong, Xicheng District	10-66085480

Kaorouji

Originally a small, local grill stand, Kaorouji has evolved into one of the most legendary restaurants in Beijing. Having fed people for over one and a half century, it is now located in a large pavilion beside Qianhai Lake. Lucky customers can sit by the window to enjoy the lakeside view, while hungrily munching their food. Also, tables are provided on fancy boats, which are especially popular amongst foreign diners. The meals are generally picked and prepared by the restaurant chefs, but, there are grill tables where diners can cook their own food as well. The restaurant offers over 160 dishes on the menu, giving famished customers a large collection to choose from. Unquestionably, the trademark dish at Kaorouji is the grilled mutton, which comes in eight different flavors. However, the menu also includes other Chinese delicacies, such as, seafood and vegetables. It is said that Kaorouji uses over 1,000 kilograms of mutton everyday during weekends, which perfectly shows the flourishing popularity of this restaurant.

Kaorouji is just beside Yinding Bridge at Shishahai

The further information of Kaorouji:

✉	14 Qianhai Dongyan, Xicheng District
☎	86-10-6404-2554
🚌	5, 60, 107 at Gulou Station
P	Avaliable
$	Approx. 80 RMB per Person
💳	Accepted

Fengzeyuan Fanzhuang

Fengzeyan Fanzhuang is absolutely one of the most legendary and celebrated restaurant is Beijing. It was first established in 1930 by the most renowned chefs in China, and to this day, Fengzeyuan's superior flavors are still stuffing the mouths of hungry customers. During the 1960s, national figureheads, such as Mao Zedong and Zhou Enlai, feasted with international guests in Fengzeyuan. Today, influential officials, noble family members, celebrities, and wealthy businessmen still enjoy banquets here. This top-class Shandong Cuisine restaurant is also separated into

The further information of Fengzeyuan:

Beijing Fengzeyuan Restaurant

✉	83 Zhushikou Xi Da Jie, Xuanwu District
☎	86-10-63186688
🚌	23, 57, 715 at Zhushikou Station
P	Avaliable
$	Approx. 160 RMB per Person
💳	Accepted

many divisions depending on interests and hobbies. Literature-loving people can choose to dine in a room with a scholarly theme, while entertainment-loving people can eat in a room full of game boards. Every dish at Fengzeyuan has a legacy of its own, and the sizzling sounds and luscious aromas will always fill the air here.

Shaguoju

Shaguoju was first established during the Qing Dynasty, and today, it is mostly recognized for its special dish – the Plain Meat in Casserole, which translates to "white-boiled meat." Dishes made with these casseroles are tender, and are complemented with specially made sauces; they come in thin slices of boiled pork on top of cabbage vegetables and noodles. After a century of culinary evolution, Shaguoju not only offers stewed pork, but also now serves chicken, fish, shrimp, crab, sea cucumber, shark fin, seashells, and many other exotic choices. This restaurant, in addition to the Plain Meat in Casserole, specializes in a unique menu, which includes Braised Crystal Ham, Tossed Pork Skin and Jelly Fish, Marinated Pork Intestine, and Meatball in Casserole.

Shaguoju Restaurant

The giant Shaguo stays in the restaurant.

The further information of Shaguoju

	60 Xisi Nan Da Jie, Xicheng District
	86-10-66061874
	22, 47 at Gangwashi Station
	Avaliable
	Approx. 60 RMB per Person
	Not accepted

Laozhengxing

Laozhengxing Restaurant is one of the oldest and most famous Shanghai cuisine restaurants in Beijing. The restaurant is located on Qianmen Street near the Old Town God Temple, and it is acknowledged for its authentic and traditional Shanghai flavor. Some of its more recognized dishes include Babao Duck, Fried Prawn and Ba Bao La Jiang.

Laozhengxing is famous for its Shanghai cuisine.

The further information of Laozhengxing:

	44 Qianmen Da Jie, Chongwen District
	86-10-67022686
	8, 120, 820 and Subway Line 2 at Qianmen Station
	Avaliable
	Approx. 40 RMB per Person
	Not accepted

Hongbinlou

Hongbinlou Restaurant

First opened in 1853, Hongbinlou Restaurant has been one of the best Muslim gourmet restaurants in Beijing for over 150 years. This restaurant is very spacious and has provided delicious banquets for many honored guests. The restaurant is adorned with Muslim decorations, and hundreds of authentic Muslim tables cover the restaurant floor. Some delicacies to look out for include Braised Shark Fin with Sliced Chicken, Stewed Sheep Head with Sauce in Casserole, Stewed Sheep Belly, and Braised Deep-fried Cattle Tail in Brown Sauce.

The further information of Hongbinlou:

✉	11 Zhanlanguan Lu, Xicheng District
☎	86-10-68992569
🚌	101, 15, 707, 709, 716, 732, 814 at Baiwanzhuang Station
P	Avaliable
💰	Approx. 80 RMB per Person
💳	Accepted

Jiumen Snack Street

Jiumen Snack Street is a popular haven for Beijing locals and tourists to gather. Actually, it is a street lined with small stands, where merchants sell Beijing's best

A corner of Jiumen Snack Street

Jiumen Snack Street is located at the bank of Houhai. The address is 1 Xiaoyou Hutong, Shishahai Houhai.

traditional snacks. Because these stands are top-class, many of the snacks are not cheap; in fact, many are quite pricey.

Wangfujing Snack Market

Wangfujing Snack Market is extremely popular for its interesting variety of Chinese food and its amazing prices. Actually, almost everything here is less than 10 US dollars. The street is busy with ambitious street vendors, curious wanderers, and numerous food stands, where they sell exotic choices of food ranging from Pekinese duck and dumplings, to even insects on sticks! The street is very lively all throughout the night.

Directions:

Two blocks north from the Orient Plaza and two blocks east from the Forbidden City.

1 Many Choices
2 The Entrance of the Snack Street
3 Just pick one you want to try. They will cook for you
4 What is this?

Following is the list of some restaurants in Beijing with different local styles in China.

Cuisines	Retaurant Name	Address	Phone No.
Guangdong Cuisine	Shunfeng Restaurant	6 Dongsanhuan Beilu, Chaoyang District	10-6502-2443
	Xin A Jing Restaurant	90 Xidan Beidajie, Xicheng District	10-6601-8288
Shandong Cuisine	Hui Feng Tang	5/F, Kuntai Mansion, Chaoyangmenwai Dajie	10-6827-1507
	Taifenglou Restaurant	2, Qianmen Xi Da Jie, Xuanwu District	10-6301-6107
Sichuan Cuisine	Taoranju	4/F, Kuntai Mansion, Chao Yangmenwai Dajie	10-6599+3323
	Feitengyuxiang	1, Gongti Bei Lu, Chaoyang District	10-6301-6107
Jiangsu Cuisine	Huaiyangcun	2/F, Tiaoqiao Hotel, Xijing Lu, Xuanwu District	10-8315-4752
	Futaigong	1~3/F, Railway Project Mansion, S. Square of W. Railway Station	10-5189-2678
Zhejiang Cuisine	Kong Yiji Restaurant	2, Dongming Hutong, Xicheng District	10-6618-4915
	Hangzhou Louwailou	71, Chaoyangmennei Beixiaojie, Dongcheng District	10-6404-9340
Fujian Cuisine	Fuzhou Hui Guan	A 30, Qianbanbi Jie, Xizhimen Area, Xicheng District	10-6618-1117
	Old Character Hakka Restaurrant	East bank of the Shishahai, Xicheng District	10-6404-2259
Hunan Cuisine	Cai Xiang Gen Restaurant	9, Yuetan Nanjie, Xicheng District	10-6241-8557
	Xiang E Qing	A 2, Dinghuisi, Fucheng Lu, Haidian District	10-8813-5488
Anhui Cuisine	Hui Cai Jiulou	3, Sidaokou, Dazhongsi, Haidian District	10-6213-9997
	Huiyuan Caifang	B1/F, Huandao Boya Hotel, No.2, Wanshou Lu, Haidian District	10-6827-3688
Xinjiang Cuisine	Uncle Afanti	166 Chaonei Dajie	10-6525-1071
	Afanti	66 Chaonei Dajie, Dongcheng District	10-6527-2288
Yunnan Cuisine	Yunnan Government Office	7, Donghuashi Beili Dongqu, Chongwen District	10-6711-3322
	Yunnan Tu Si Cai	Guangqumen Donglu, Chaoyang District	10-6773-0556
Tibetan Cuisine	Makye Ame	A11 Xiushui Nanjie, Jianguomenwai, Chaoyang District	10-6506-9616
	An Abiding Flower of Prosperity	2nd Floor, Commercial Building, Xingfu Er Cun, Chaoyang District	10-6417-9269
Taiwan Cuisine	An Ping Ancient Street	39 E.3rd Ring M. Rd., Chaoyang District	10-5869-2083
	Bellagio	35, Xiaoyunlu, Chaoyang District	10-8451-9988
Hakka Cuisine	Kejia Cai	Southeast bank of Qian Hai	10-6404-2259
	Lao Hanzi	Shishahai East Bank	10-6404-2259
Vegetarian	Green Tianshi Vegetarian	57 Dengshikou Street, Dongcheng District	10-6524-2349
	Gongdelin	58 Qianmen Nan Da Jie, Chongwen District	10-6702-0867

World Cuisine

Country	Restaurant	Address	Phone	Average Cost Per Person
India	Shamiana	98 Beilishi Lu, Xicheng District (inside Holiday Inn)	10-6833-8822	200-300 CNY
	Asian Star	26 East Third Ring North Road	10-6582-5306	100-200 CNY
Japan	Genji	1 Dong Fang Road, North 3rd Ring Road, (inside Hilton Hotel)	10-6466-2288 ext. 7402	100-300 CNY
	Kiku Yo	3 Tuanjiehu North Side	10-6582-2007	100-200 CNY
France	Plaza Grill	48 Wangfujing Da Jie (2/F, Rainbow Plaza)	10-6513-3388 ext. 1132	700-800 CNY
	Flo	16 East Third Ring Road (2/F, Rainbow Plaza)	10-6595-5139 /5140	200-300 CNY
Italia	Annie's Cafe	West Gate of Chaoyang Park	10-6591-1931	100-200 CNY
	Metro Cafe	6 West Gongti Lu, Chaoyang District	10-6552-7828	100-200 CNY
German	Kebab Cafe	Sanlitun North Street	10-6415-5812	100-200 CNY
	Schiller's	1 Liangmahe South Road, opposite Jingcheng Mansion	10-6464-9016	100-200 CNY

After gulping down all that Chinese food, you might find yourself longing for some flavors of your home town. Not only does Beijing have hundreds of foreign restaurants, many of them are mirror images of the food you'll find at home. Beijing restaurants essentially offer dishes from every corner of the globe, and there are many of the well-known fast food restaurants here as well. Whether you are craving the juicy steaks of American cooking or the fresh sushi from Japanese cuisines, Beijing offers every taste for every picky customer.

Country	Restaurant	Address	Phone	Average Cost Per Person
America	Courtyard	95 Donghuamen Da Jie, Dongcheng District	10-6526-8883	150-250 CNY
	Tim's Texas Bar-B-Q	14 Dongdaqiao Lu, Suite 2, Chaoyang District	10-6591-9161	100-200 CNY
Russia	Moscow Restaurant	135 Xi Zhimen Wai Da Jie, Beside Beijing Exhibition Center	10-6835-4454	100-150 CNY
	Traktirr	A1 Xiyangguan Hutong, Beizhong Jie, Dongzhimen Nei Da Jie	10-6403-1896	100-200 CNY
Brazil	Rio Brazilian BBQ	Building 5, 9-13, Dongzhimen Nei Da Jie	10-8406-4368	150-200 CNY
	Alamede	Sanlitun Beijie, Chaoyang District, 80 M.south of 3.3 Shopping	10-6417-8084	100-200 CNY
Swiss	Souk	West entrance of Chaoyang Park, Chaoyang District	10-6506-7309	100-150 CNY
	Morel's	5 Xinzhong Jie, Chaoyang District	10-6416-8802	80-180 CNY
Thai	Pink Loft	6 Sanlitun Nan Lu, Chaoyang District	10-6506-8811	100-150 CNY
	Lemon Leaf	15 Xiaoyun Lu, Chaoyang District	10-6462-5505	100-200 CNY

Sleep should not be at the top of your priority list when vacationing in Beijing. Beijing nightlife offers almost EVERY sort of entertainment that will procrastinate your mind from worries.

Beijing hotels offer an assortment of luxuries, from bars, billiards, and pools to parties, massages, saunas, and karaokes – you name it, they have it. Of course, you should not restrict your evening to hotels. Considered to be a large melting pot, Beijing streets are filled with restaurants and bars. Street entertainers and various bands also presents nightly performances in the downtown Beijing area.

Chapter 6

Beijing Nightlife

6-1

Theaters

National Grand Theater

Completed at the end of 2007, the National Grand Theater (Chinese: 国家大剧院), or "The Egg" by reputation, is one of the most renowned architectural feats of modern China. An ellipsoid dome of titanium and glass, this opera house is located near an artificial lake, and the combination of the dome and reflection offers an image of an egg. The theatre covers over 200,000 sq. meters, and it houses 6,500 seats and three different halls. Used for operas, ballets, plays, and dances, the Opera Hall seats 2,416, the Music Hall 2,017 and the Theater Hall 1,040. Designed by French architect Pau Andreu, the National Grand Theater is located at the heart of Beijing and is a cultural haven for entertainment.

Picture of National Grand Theater

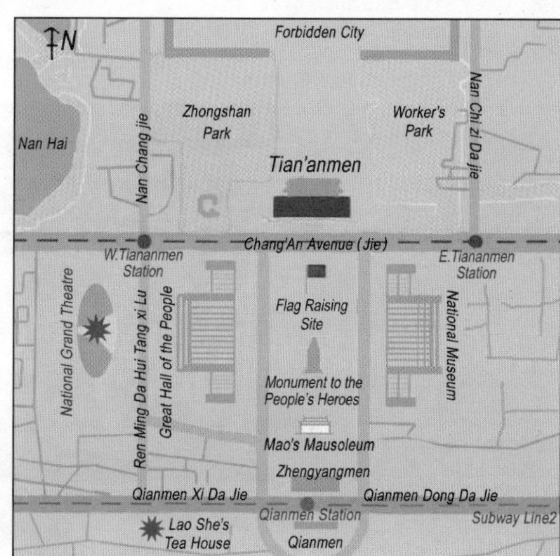

Map of National Grand Theater & Lao She's Tea House

Lao She's Teahouse

Lao She (1899-1966), real name Shu Qingchun, was a legendary author and playwright of China. Born as a Manchurian decent, Lao She accomplished many feats in his life time, such as writing the book *Camel Xiangzi*. Known in the US as the Rickshaw, this book became one of the era's best sellers. During his early years, Lao She taught English at Oriental School of London University and eventually wrote

The Entrance of Laoshe's Teahouse

many works, including *City of Cats*, *The Yellow Storm*, and *The Drum Singers*. However, Lao She is most renowned for his drama *Tea House*, which was written in 1957. During the Cultural Revolution, public criticism and denouncements unfortunately drove Lao She to suicide on August 24, 1966.

Lao She's Teahouse was built in 1988 and is named exactly after Lao She's famous drama. Today, it has evolved into a superb entertainment house with performances by comedians, singers, musicians, acrobats and opera performers. The teahouse is a motley of Beijing flavor and culture, and the furniture and decorations give a taste of stylishness and elegance. Affordable dinners

Model of Lao She's Teahouse

Inside of Lao She's Teahhouse

are offered for visitors, and tourists can enjoy prime examples of Chinese art and literature, while sipping their soothing tea.

Lao She's Teahouse is located at Qianmen Xi Da Jie Building #3. In general, the price ranges from 60 to 180 CNY to drink tea and watch a performance.

Phone number: 10-6302-1717.

Chang'an Grand Theater

The front of Chang'an Grand Theater

Located on Chang'an Avenue, the Chang'an Grand Theater is a famous Beijing opera house that holds high-level performances. This modern theater is a place where people can come and experience a festive time. From music to martial arts, this grand theater showcases a wide-range of traditional Chinese history, culture, and mythology. However, this 800-seat opera house is most renowned for its Peking Opera, also called Jingju. There is a monument designed like the facial makeup of opera singers at the entrance. The colorful costumes, facial makeup, musical dialogues, and grand settings make the Chang'an Grand Theater's performances a must-see attraction.

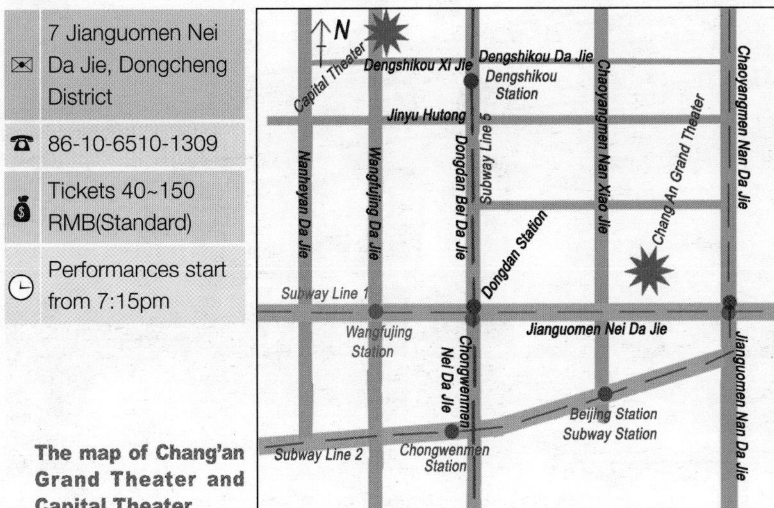

The map of Chang'an Grand Theater and Capital Theater

Beijing People's Art Theater

For decades, China's most prestigious drama company has been the Beijing People's Art Theater. Similar to Broadway, the actors' first-class performances have left many legacies across the globe, and since 1980's, the theater has put on over 80 different plays. The theater, in 1904, was the first in China to put on huaju – or spoken drama – which was adopted from western styles. Since its founding, the theater has put on over 300 plays of different styles, themes, and settings; some plays include *Wang Zhaojun*, *Warning Signals*, *Xiao Jing Hutong*, *Weddings and Funerals*, *Uncle Doggie's Nirvana*, and some of these have been performed over 100 times. The diverse repertoire offers a superb range of rigorous stagecraft, artistic style, and emotional depth, and the theater has been famous for producing generations of talented actors and actresses. The theater company performs in three theaters: the Capital Theater, the Mini Theater, and the Experimental Theater. Today, Beijing People's Art Theater has received a huge boost and is starting to perform in China's National Theater. The People's theater's major success is unquestionably ready to astound all audiences.

Capital Theater is located on 22 Wangfujing Da Jie and the phone number is 10-6525-0123.

Former Performance Place: Capital Theater

On the front of Huguang Theater

Hu Guang Guild Hall Theater

Beijing Hu Guang Guild Hall (Hu Guang Hui Guan) is easily identified by its traditional style of curved roofs and decorated tiles. Constructed during the reign of Jiaqing (1807), this guild hall used to hold performances of famous opera prodigies, such as Tan Xinpei (谭鑫培), Yu Shuyan (于叔岩) and Mei Lanfang (梅兰芳). On August 25, 1912, the "Father of Modern China" Sun Yat-sen held a meeting at the Beijing Hu Guang Guild Hall; this marked the day of Kuomintang Party's founding. The guild hall, now, also receives academic discussions and caterings as well. Inside, there are colorful birds, luscious flowers, and artistic pavilions. The guild hall houses the Exhibition Hall of Traditional Opera

A Peking Opera performance

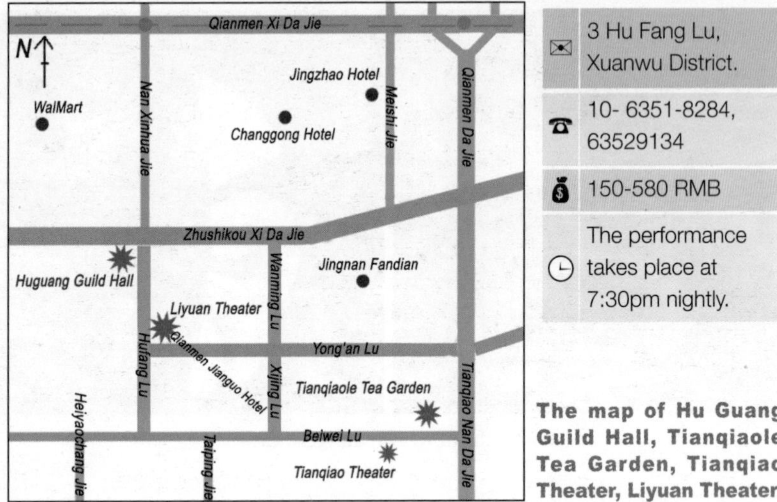

3 Hu Fang Lu, Xuanwu District.

10- 6351-8284, 63529134

150-580 RMB

The performance takes place at 7:30pm nightly.

The map of Hu Guang Guild Hall, Tianqiaole Tea Garden, Tianqiao Theater, Liyuan Theater

Museum in Beijing, and it provides tea tables along with an intimate atmosphere for any tourist or visitor. The museum showcases photos of famous opera singers in addition to old opera gowns; visitors can also view the adroitly refurbished theater with a decorated traditional stage and gallery seating. Every Saturday and Sunday, many theatergoers and opera masters come to give special performances that truly shine a light upon Beijing's traditions and culture.

Tianqiaole Tea Garden, Tianqiao Theater & Liyuan Theater

Tianqiao (Overbridge) Area is one of the unique attractions that tourists should not miss out on. Although named as a bridge, Tianqiao Area is actually a popular mecca for gatherings, delicious foods and beverages, and entertainment. Since the Yuan Dynasty, this popular location has epitomized Chinese entertainment, from acrobats to music.

Liyuan Theater is a traditional Chinese Performance stage located inside Qianmen Jianguo Hotel. Beijing Operas and regional folk groups perform nightly, and to the benefit of most visitors, these dramas primarily engage audiences through mimes. Operas often have subtitle boards presenting translations; these luxuries ensure that language barriers will not interfere with

The Entrance of Tianqiaole Tea Garden

Tianqiaole Tea Garden is famous for traditional arts of Peking Opera, acrobatics, martial Arts and folk songs.

✉	1 Beiwei Lu (just west of intersection with Qianmen Da Jie).
☎	86-10-6304-0617
$	150-330 RMB(with Dinner)

Tianqiao Theater

Tianqiao Theater specializes in modern music and dance performances.

✉	No. 21 Beiwei Lu, Xuanwu District
☎	86-10-83156170 /83156172
$	80-880 RMB

the overall experience.

To add to the excitement of the performances, you can visit the makeup rooms to witness firsthand the professional actors adorning themselves with exquisite makeup. Also, you can get autographs and pictures with actors after performances. For those interested in background information, the exhibition hall offers the history of Peking Opera along with photos of famous actors and artists. The wonderful experience at the Liyuan Theater can be remembered forever with a small purchase at the souvenir shop. Selling traditional facial makeup, musical instruments, calligraphy, paintings,

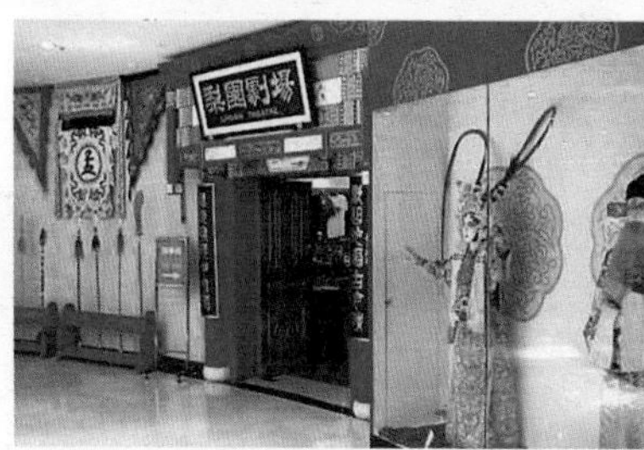

Liyuan Theater

The performers are putting on their exquisite makeup

✉	Every evening at 7:30pm
☎	175 Yong'an Lu (Inside Qianmen Jianguo Hotel), Xuanwu District
💰	280-480 RMB

Beijing Night Show

Beijing Night Show is a 90-minute performance located in a grandeur theater in Dayabao Hutong, Dongcheng District. Dedicated to Chinese culture, history and tradition, the performances illustrate today's civilization through dances, music and banquets. Also, visitors can marvel upon the adept entertainers' kungfu and acrobatic expertise; the addition of ethnic customs, cultural costumes, and operas creates another dimension for audiences and actors alike. In the first half of the show, you can also have dinner inside the theater to complete your experience; this banquet offers an exquisite collection of Chinese delicacies from different eras of Chinese history. The lifelike range of Chinese artistic performances makes Beijing Night Show the spotlight of attention for theatergoers.

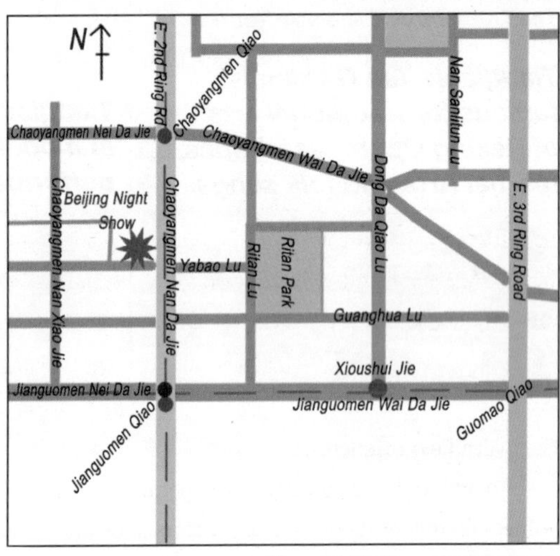

Map of Beijing Night Show

✉	1 Dayabao Hutong, Dongcheng District
☎	86-10-6527-2814
🕒	19:00-21:30
💰	280-680 RMB (with Dinner)

6-2
Bars

Beijing streets are famous for their colossal collection of bars. Ranging in cultures and nationalities, bars are essentially found almost everywhere, including dance clubs, pubs, coffee houses, music clubs, entertainment clubs, and art clubs. Following is a guide of Beijing night life in bars.

Sanlitun Area

In Chaoyang District near the international embassies, Sanlitun is a highly popular street filled with tourists year-round. After a simple walk down this street, you would pass over 100 bars on both sides. Sanlitun is unquestionably the most vivacious site, where live bands, night clubs, karaokes, and other forms of entertainment fill the night air.

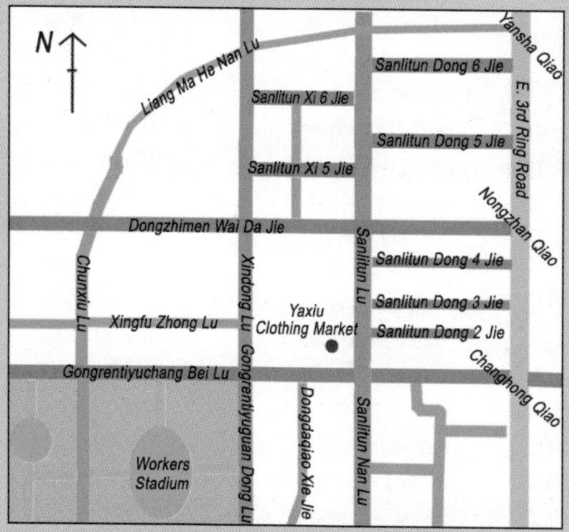

Sanlitun Area Map

The Sign of Sanlitun Lu

A bar on the side of Sanlitun Lu

A Bar called "Yangguang" is on 22 Sanlitun Lu.

The List of Some Bars Around Sanlitun Area:

	Name		Address	Phone No
1	Boys & Girls	男孩女孩	68 Sanlitun Bei Jie	10-6416-6777
2	NO. 52	52 号	52 Sanlitun Bei Jie	10-6416-4697
3	EASYPUB	简单日子	36 Sanlitun Bei Jie	10-6417-6886
5	DESSY BAR	戴茜小屋	48 Sanlitun Xi Jie	10-6416-4034
6	JAZZ YA	爵士屋	18 Sanlitun Bei Jie	10-6415-1227
7	Da Chuan	大船酒吧	8 Sanlitun Bei Jie	10-6416-1633
8	SkYLINE	地平线	70 Sanlitun Bei Jie	10-6415-1558
9	LAN KWUI FANG	兰桂坊	66 Sanlitun Bei Jie	10-6417-2589
10	MILAN CLUB	米兰俱乐部	62 Sanlitun Bei Jie	10-6416-4560
11	COMMA BAR	逗号	54 Sanlitun Bei Jie	10-6417-4643
12	SWING	云胜	58 Sanlitun Bei Jie	10-6415-9196
13	INNER AFFAIR		6 Sanlitun Xi Jie	10-8454-0899
14	Downtown	骊姿园	26 Sanlitun Bei Jie	10-6415-2100
15	PALM BEACH	棕榈海滩	56 Sanlitun Bei Jie	10-6416-4191
16	PRETTY LILY	靓丽百合	46 Sanlitun Bei Jie	10-6417-5985
17	Red Moon Club	月色交友	8 Sanlitun Bei Jie	10-6416-6613
18	The Tree	树	43 Sanlitun Bei Jie	10-6415-1954
19	Serve the People	为人民服务	1 Sanlitun Xi Wu Jie	10-8454-4580
20	ASSAGGI	尝试	1 Sanlitun Bei Xiao Jie	10-8454-4508
21	Athena	雅典娜	1 Sanlitun Xi Wu Jie	10-6464-6036
22	ALAMEDA	ALAMEDA	Sanlitun Bei Li	10-6417-8084
23	Gold Barn	金谷仓	1 Sanlitun Bei Jie	10-6463-7240
24	Golden Elephant	金象东方	Building 7, Sanlitun Bei Li	10-6417-1650
25	Hidden Tree	隐蔽的树	Behind Yaxiu Macket, Sanlitun	10-6415-1954

Shishahai

Lie Huo Feng Huang

With a history of over 700 years, Shishahai is Beijing's largest commercial area surrounding lakes. Bars are scattered all around the water, and tourists leisurely drink martinis, while enjoying the lake-side view. Shishahai is especially recognized for its poetic beauty, and at night, red candles are set free onto the lake waters to create a dreamy atmosphere.

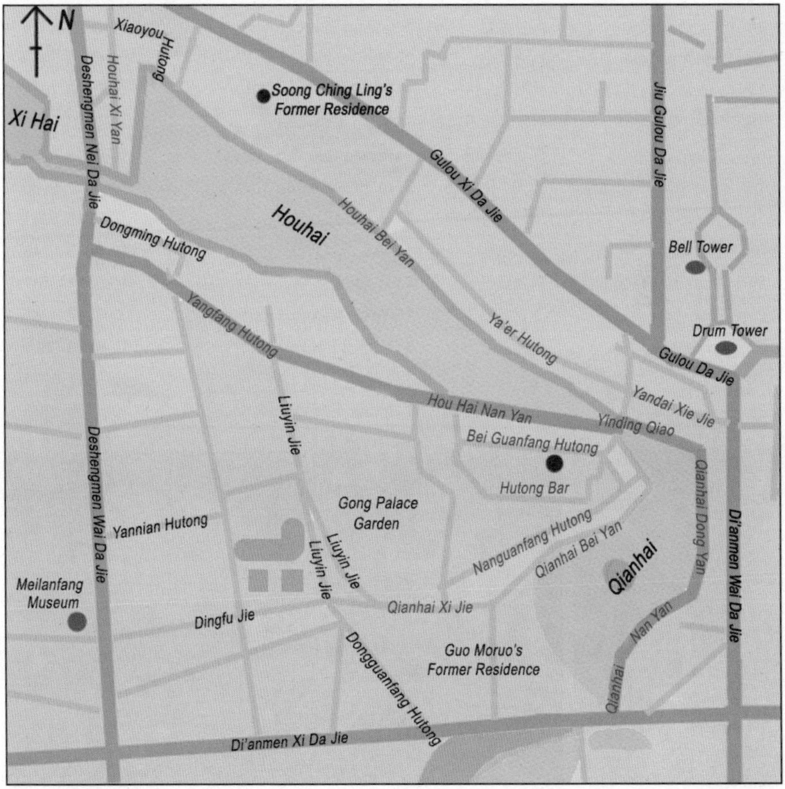

Map of Shishahai Area

The List of Some Bars in Shishahai Area:

	Name		Address	Phone No.
1	La Baie Des Anges	天使港湾	5 Nan Guanfang Hutong, Houhai	10-6657-1065
2	Golder Titian		83 Yandai Xie Jie	10-8404-7171
3	Club Nuage	云上	22 Qianhai Dong Yan	10-6404-6870
4	Buddha	老祁酒吧	2 Yindingqiao, Houhai	10-6617-9418
5	No Name Bar	无名酒吧	3 Qianhai Dong Yan	10-6401-8541
6	The Thirty One Bar	三十一酒吧	16 Houhai Nan Yan	10-6616-4210
7	Hui Xian Tan	会贤坛	13 Qianhai Bei Yan	10-6617-6221
8	Wang Hai Yi Ran	望海怡然	6 Houhai Nan Yan	10-6612-0239
9	Sampan Bar	舢板酒吧	1 Qianhai Bei Yan	10-6611-8558
10		百龄碧浪	6 Ya'er Hutong,Houhai	10-8400-2085
11	Camrang	春荣酒吧	37 Bei Guanfnag Hutong , Houhai	10-6613-5689
12		依绿棕酒吧	16 Houhai Nan Yan	10-6611-7213
13		闻进酒吧	4 Yinding Qiao, Houhai	10-6618-4823
14	Houhai Café	后海酒吧	20 Houhai Nan Yan	10-6613-6209
15	Zone	佐酒吧	12 Houhai Xi Yan	10-8403-1419
16	Yun Ya Bar	运雅酒吧	85 Yandai Xie Jie	10-6403-6588
17	Chao Long Ge	潮泷阁酒吧	4 Houhai Nan Yan	10-6618-6270
18	Lie Huo Feng Huang	烈火凤凰酒吧	6 Houhai Nan Yan	10-6612-5886
19	Hutong Bar	胡同写意酒吧	8 Houhai Nan Yan	10-6615-8691
20	Buddha	老祁酒吧 2	16 Yinding Qiao, Houhai	10-6615-5746
21	Nan Jiu Wang Dan	南九旺丹	4 Houahi Bei Yan	10-6651-0187
22	Buddha	老祁酒吧 3	18 Yinding Qiao, Houhai	10-6417-9488
23	Touch	接触酒吧	8 Qianhai Bei Yan	10-6618-0809
24		经典碧浪	13 Qianhai Bei Yan	10-6617-6221
25		半打啤酒屋	2 Houhai Bei Yan	10-6406-4935

Zone Bar

Hutong Bar

Xing Bar Lu & Lucky Street

Xing Bar Lu is a street full of restaurants, bars and entertainment. With over 30 bars seating over 700 people, this street attracts many of China's rock bands, such as Zheng Jun and Cui Jian, China's granddaddy of rock and roll and improvisation.

Lately, Lucky Street (好运街) – a newly-developed area – has become a popular attraction. This 260-meter-long street is located just south of Xing Bar Lu and is filled with restaurants, bars, clubs and brand name shops.

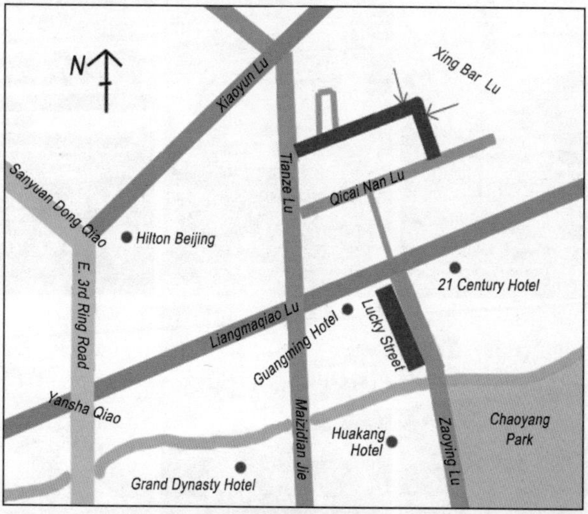

N
Xiaoyun Lu
Xing Bar Lu
Tianze Lu
Qicai Nan Lu
Sanyuan Dong Qiao
Hilton Beijing
E. 3rd Ring Road
21 Century Hotel
Liangmaqiao Lu
Guangming Hotel
Lucky Street
Yansha Qiao
Maizidian Jie
Zaoying Lu
Chaoyang Park
Huakang Hotel
Grand Dynasty Hotel

Map of Xing Bar Lu and Lucky Street

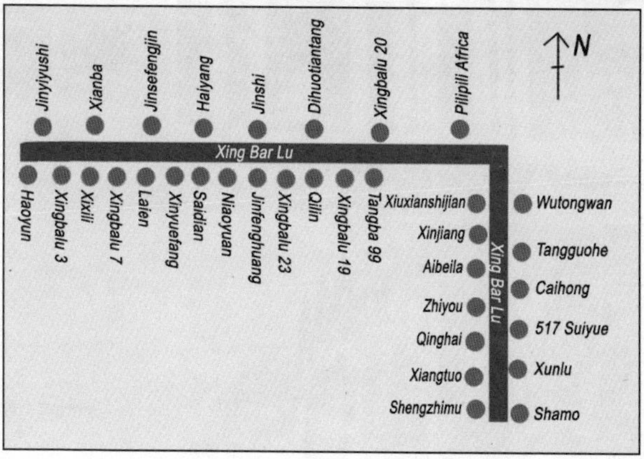

Jinyiyushi
Xianba
Jinsefengjin
Haiyang
Jinshi
Dihuotiantang
Xingbalu 20
Pilipili Africa
N
Xing Bar Lu
Haoyun
Xingbalu 3
Xixili
Xingbalu 7
Laien
Xinyuefang
Saidian
Niaoyuan
Jinfenghuang
Xingbalu 23
Qilin
Xingbalu 19
Tangba 99
Xiuxianshijian
Xinjiang
Aibeila
Zhiyou
Qinghai
Xiangtuo
Shengzhimu
Xing Bar Lu
Wutongwan
Tangguohe
Caihong
517 Suiyue
Xunlu
Shamo

Bars on Xing Bar Lu

Shops on Lucky Street

Chapter 7

Shopping

From antiques to modern merchandise, brand name products to counterfeits, Beijing markets have them all. Tourists have always considered Beijing to be a treasure cave, selling products of every purpose, brand and function. To many people, these markets are also centers for haggling; obeying the laws of supply and demand, merchants and customers treat the Beijing markets as a bargaining arena. Numerous shopping centers offer entertainment as well, including bands and fashion shows. SOGO and Chung-yo are examples of traditional shopping centers, while Wangfujing and Xidan are Beijing's newly-renovated modern malls. Of course, you can also take a shot at the countless vendors out in the open-air market.

7-1 Wangfujing Business Street

Wangfujing is Beijing's most famous and historic market place. Although this street is only one kilometer long, it is lined with stores and countless people. The most established store here is the Beijing Department Store, but others include the largest arts and crafts shop, Dong'an Market, the largest Xinhua Bookstore, the newly-made and largest store-Oriental Plaza, and many, many more. Shops from different countries can be found here as well. Basically, you can shop forever, or, at least until your wallet turns empty!

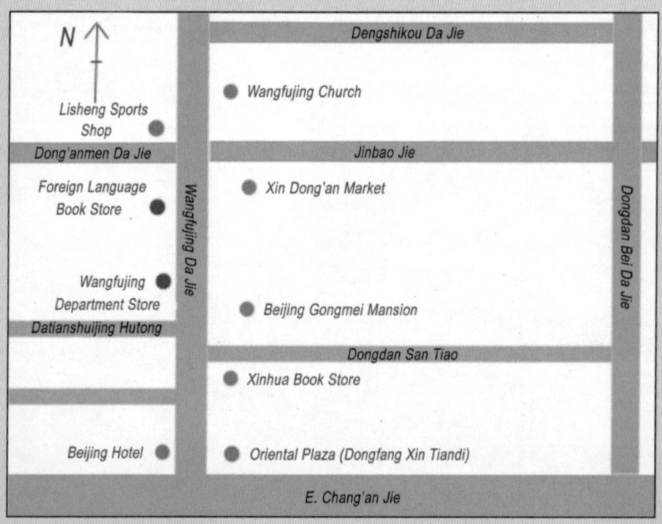

Map of Wangfujing Street

Wangfujing Street

Oriental Plaza

Foreign Language Book Store

7-2 Xidan Business Street

Xidan is a very large market place, similar to Wangfujing. Located very close to Tian'anmen Square, Xidan is a shopping mecca for more Beijing residents than tourists. There are many malls that are similar to multi-level department stores found in United States. Consumer goods of every kind, such as electronics, clothing and food, are sold here at cheaper prices than those at Wangfujing. The Grand Pacific is one of the largest department stores in Beijing,

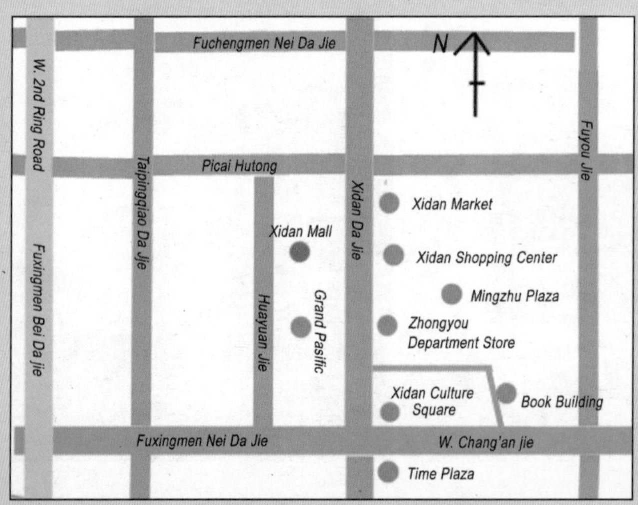

Map of Xidan Shopping Area

Shopping in Xidan Mall

Time Plaza in Xidan

and it exclusively sells fashionable products. Also, stores in the subway are opening; due to the variety of fashionable options, Xidan is very popular among the younger generations. Time Plaza is the most expensive store, selling high priced brand name products; because of this, this store is most likely the least-crowded store at Xidan.

Crowded Xidan

7-3

Silk Market

Unlike what its name says, the Silk Market offers a lot more than just silk. Selling cashmere garments, jackets, leather goods, shoes, hats, watches and souvenirs of brand name companies or counterfeits, this market is the haven for bargaining. Anyone shopping here should immediately haggle with a starting price of at least 50-70% of the original. If merchants remain stubborn, do not be afraid to simply walk away because there are many other vendors selling the exact same product. Most likely, the stubborn merchant will call you back anyway. The Silk Market is a perfect location for tourists who are interested in Chinese markets; most people are fairly fluent with English too. Just keep an eye out for persuasive vendors and counterfeit goods!

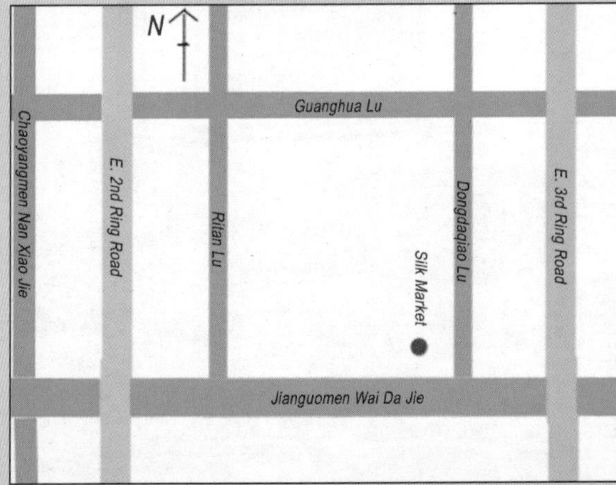

Map of Silk Market

Silk Market was formally located on the streets. Today, it is located in this large building.

Inside Silk Market

7-4 Yaxiu Market

Located on Sanlitun Lu near the embassies, the Yaxiu Market is similar to the Silk Market. With not quite as many counterfeits, this location is an indoor four-story store that especially specializes in clothing. Full of designer goods along with some souvenirs and such, Yaxiu Market hires skilled tailors who measure and fit you with genuine made-to-order Chinese clothing, which can be completed in one or two days. The market is open daily from 9:30am to 9:00pm.

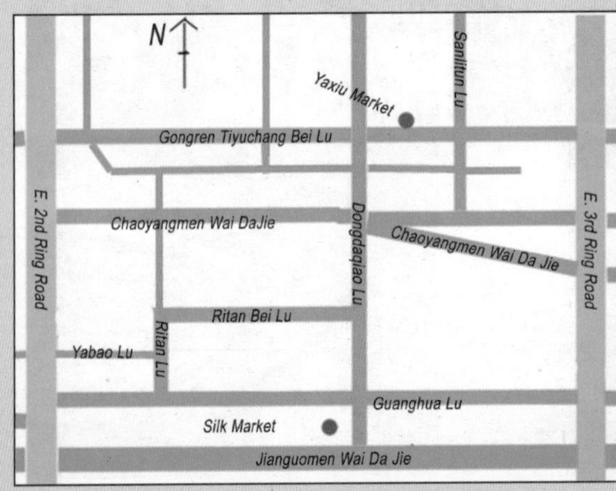

Map of Yaxiu Market

Yaxiu Market

Inside Yaxiu Maket

Making your own Chinese Dress

7-5

Dashila Street

Dashila has over 500 years of history, dating back all the way to the Ming Dynasty. Known as the "essence of Beijing," it houses many stores that have retained the look of ancient China. Dashila literally translates to "the Great Fence," and that is because Beijing, at one point, was under strict curfews, which were enforced by barriers and fences. Today, Dashila's stores are recognized for their pursuit of reputation and high quality. The pronounciation of this three Chinese Words, 大 栅 栏 is "Dazhalan", but Beijing locals call this market as "Dashila."

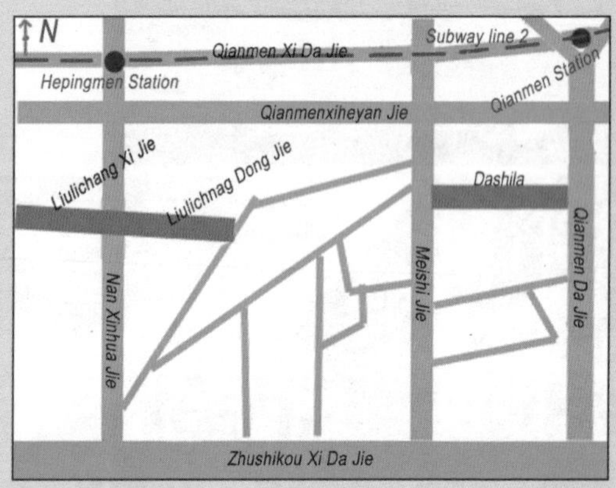

Map of Dashila

Dashila Street View

Big Fence of Dashila Street

Beijing's Time-Honored Brands in Dashila Street

7-6 Liulichang

The famous Liulichang street has existed since the Qing Dynasty. All throughout Ming and Qing Dynasties, Liulichang was a gathering site for scholars, painters and calligraphers to write, compile and exchange each other's works. It was the location where those who failed the imperial examination exchanged old study books and inkslabs. Later, Liulichang slowly evolved into a market place for traditional Chinese paintings, old wood block-print books, Chinese ink brushes, inkslabs, paper, and calligraphy. Today, there are over 100 stores dedicated to selling these various articles and antiques. Rongbaozhai (荣宝斋), which has with-stood 300 years of history, is now the prominent store on Liulichan Street.

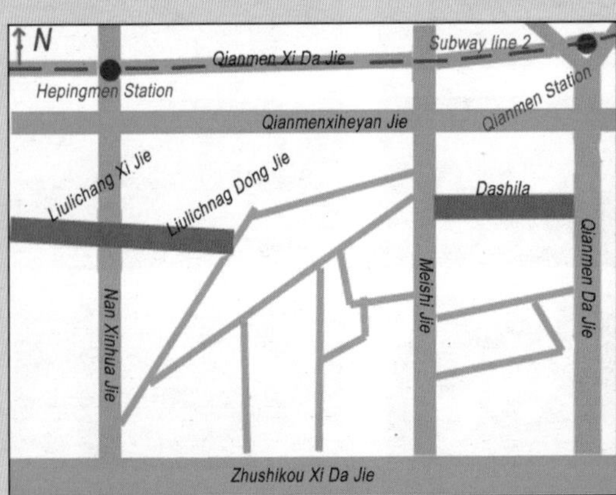

Map of Liulichang

Liulichang Street View

Sales Booths

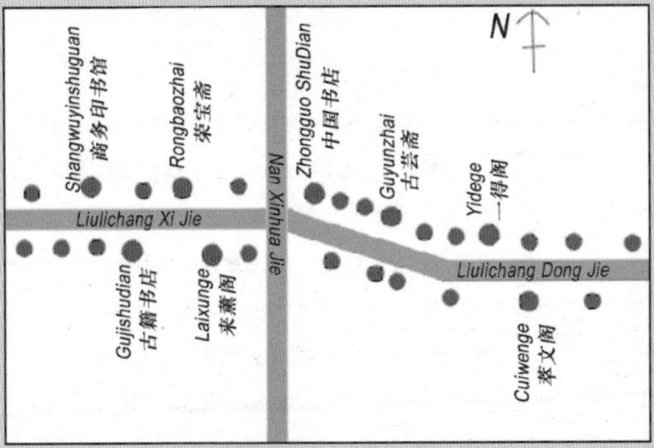

N
Shangwuyinshuguan 商务印书馆
Rongbaozhai 荣宝斋
Zhongguo ShuDian 中国书店
Guyunzhai 古芸斋
Yidege 一得阁
Liulichang Xi Jie
Nan Xinhua Jie
Liulichang Dong Jie
Gujishudian 古籍书店
Laixunge 来薰阁
Cuiwenge 萃文阁

Historic Shops on Liulichang Street

Rongbaozhai

7-7

Flea Market - Panjiayuan

Beijing's flea market has one of the most assorted collections of products. Nicknamed the "Dirt Market," the flea market is only open during weekends, where hundreds of merchants come to display their interesting goods. Ranging from instruments, pictures, and utensils to antiques, pottery, and even door knobs, this "Dirt Market" literally sells some of everything. The variety does include some materials, which you may consider "trash" but the high numbers of customers make this flea market a festive location. A good taste of a Beijing business can be obtained here as long as you are alert for any scams.

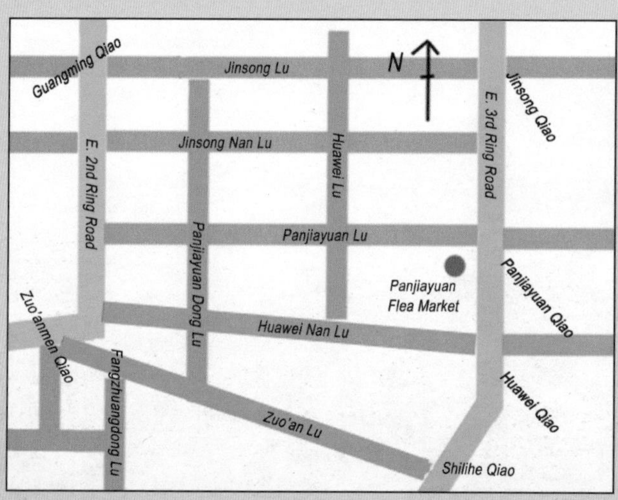

Open-air Market

Busy Market

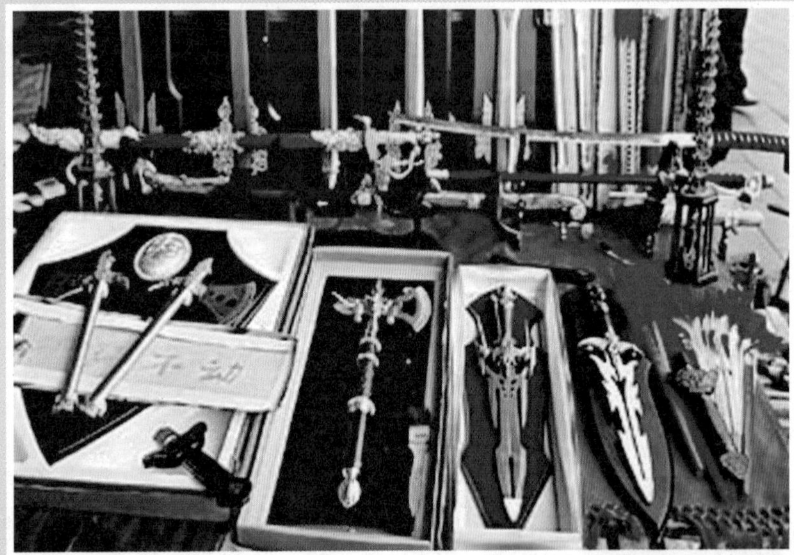

Prices can be one-fifth of US prices

Relics or Counterfeits?

Chapter 8

Beijing Olympic Games

8-1 About Beijing Olympic Games 2008

On August 8, 2008, the XXIX Olympics are to commence at 8pm and 8 seconds in Beijing. Construction companies and committees have prepared for this extraordinary moment in history. In Haidan District, the Olympic Green is a forest park where many major arenas, stadiums and the Olympic Village are located. Some of these establishments include: Beijing National Stadium, Beijing National Aquatics Centre, Beijing National Indoor Stadium, Olympic Green Convention Centre, Olympic Green Hockey Field, Olympic Green Archery Field, and Olympic Green Tennis Centre.

The date of the 2008 Olympics is scheduled at a very special time under China's calendar. The number "eight" is pronounced "BA," which just so happens to rhyme with the word FA (发). In Chinese, FA means prosperity, success, and wealth, which can be frequently heard in the Chinese New Year's saying "Gong xi FA Cai" (恭喜发财). The date and time, 8/8/2008 at 8:08, of the Olympics is considered to have a lucky value under Chinese beliefs.

The Olympics will hold 623 competition sessions in the 302 events. Over 10,500 ambitious athletes will battle to obtain the international and immortal fame awaiting them in the city of Beijing.

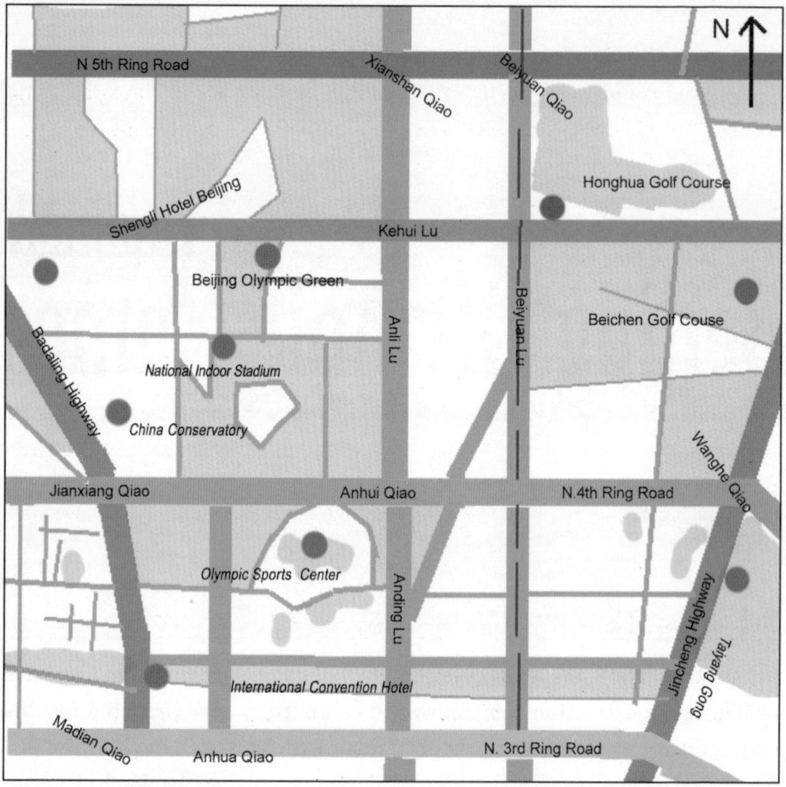

Main 2008 Summer Olympic Area

The Office of Beijing Organizing Committee for the Games of the XXIX Olympiad

Beijing Olympic Tower,

267 Beisihuan Zhong Lu (Middle Section of N.4th Ring Road),

Haidian District, Beijing, 100083, P.R. China

Tel:86-10-66692008

Fax:86-10-66699229

For more information and updates check:

http://en.beijing2008.cn

8-2 Venues of the Olympic Games

There are a total of 37 venues that will be used for competitions during the 29th Beijing Olympiad, 31 of which are in Beijing and 6 of which are outside the city.

Venues in Beijing

National Stadium

- Olympic Green, Beijing
- Athletics, Football

National Aquatics Center

- Olympic Green, Beijing
- Swimming, Diving and Synchronized Swimming

National Indoor Stadium

- Olympic Green, Beijing
- Artistic Gymnastics, Trampolines & Handball

Tennis Center

- Olympic Green, Beijing
- Tennis

Fencing Hall

- National Convention Center, Olympic Green, Beijing
- Fencing Preliminaries and Finals, Modern Pentathlon (fencing and Shooting)

Hockey Field

- Olympic Green, Beijing
- Hockey

Archery Field

- Olympic Green, Beijing
- Archery

Beijing University of Technology Gymnasium

- 100 Pingleyuan, Beijing University of Technology, Chaoyang District
- Badminton, Rhythmic Gymnastics

Olympic Sports Center Stadium

- Southern part of Olympic Sports Center, Chaoyang District
- Football, Modern Pentathlon

Olympic Sports Center Gymnasium

- 1 Anding Lu, Olympic Sports Center, Chaoyang District
- Handball

Worker's Indoor Gymnasium

- Gongti Beilu, Chaoyang District
- Boxing

Worker's Stadium

- Gongti Beilu, Chaoyang District
- Football

Yingdong Natatorium

- 1 Anding Lu, Olympic Sports Center, Chaoyang District
- Water Polo, Modern Pentathlon (Swimming)

Beach Volleyball Ground

- 1 Chaoyang Gongyuan Nan Lu, Chaoyang District

Beach Volleyball

Wukesong Basketball Gymnasium

69 Fuxing Lu, Wukesong Culture and Sports Center, Haidian District

Basketball

Laoshan Velodrome

15 Laoshan Xi Lu, Shijinshan District

Cycling

China Agricultural University Gymnasium

2 Yuanmingyuan Xi Lu, China Agricultural University (East Campus), Haidian District

Wrestling

Beijing University Gymnasium

5 Haidian Lu, Beijing University, Haidian District

Table Tennis

Beijing Science and Technology University Gymnasium

30 Xueyuan Lu, University of Science and Technology, Haidian District

Judo, Tae kwon do

Capital Indoor Stadium

5 Baishi Qiao, Haidian District

Volleyball

Beijing Shooting Range CTF

Xiang Shan Nan Lu, Haidian District

Shooting

Beijing Institute of technology Gymnasium

5 Zhongguancun Nan Da Jie, Haidian District

Volleyball

Beijing University of Aeronautics & Astronautics Gymnasium

37 Xueyuan Lu, Haidian District

Weightlifting

Wukesong Baseball Field

69 Fuxing Lu, Wukesong Culture & Sports Center, Haidian District

Baseball

Beijing Shooting Range Hall

A3 Futiansi, Shijingshan District

Shooting

Laoshan Mountain Bike Course

15 Laoshan Xi Lu, Shijingshan District

Cycling (Mountain Bike)

Laoshan Bicycle Moto Cross(BMX) Venue

15 Laoshan Xi lu, Shijingshan District

Cycling (BMX)

Fengtai Softball Field

Fengtai Sports Center, S.55 W.4th Ring Road, Fengtai District

Softball

Shunyi Olympic Rowing-Canoeing Park

Mapo Village, Shunyi District

Rowing, Canoe/Kayak -Flat-water, Canoe/Kayak - Slalom, Marathon Swimming

Triathlon Venue

Ming Tombs Reservoir, Changping District

Triathlon

Urban Road Cycling Course

Yongdingmen-Juyongguan

Cycling (race)

The Beijing Transit Company is planning on 34 new bus routes specifically for transporting Olympic participants from one arena to the next.

For 2 CNY, a one-day ticket can be purchased for the new bus routes.

Non-Beijing Venues

Hong Kong Equestrian Venues

Sha tin & Beas River, Hong Kong

Equestrian

Qingdao Olympic Sailing Center

Fushanwan, Qingdao

Sailing

Qinhuangdao Olympic Sports Center Stadium

Hebei Da Jie West, Haigang District, Qinhuangdao

Football Preliminary

Shanghai Stadium

666 Tianyaoqiao Lu, Shanghai

Football Preliminary

Shenyang Olympic Stadium

30 Hunan Zhong Lu, Shenyang

Football Preliminary

Tianjin Olympic Center StadiumTriathlon Venue

Tianjin

Football Preliminary

8-3 History of Olympics

Olympic history

Summer Olympic				Winter Olympic			
No.	Year	City	Country	No.	Year	City	Country
1	1896	Athens	Greece				
2	1900	Paris	France				
3	1904	St. Louis	USA			* 1–cancelled because of World War I * 2–cancelled because of World War II * 3–cancelled because of World War II	
4	1908	London	UK				
5	1912	Stockholm	Sweden				
*6	1916	Berlin–1	Germany				
7	1920	Antverp	Belgium				
8	1924	Paris	France	1	1924	Chamoniz	France
9	1928	Amsterdam	Netherlands	2	1928	St. Moritz	Switzerland
10	1932	Los Angeles	USA	3	1932	Lake Placid	USA

Summer Olympic				Winter Olympic			
11	1936	Berlin	Germany	4	1936	Garmisch-Partenkirchen	Germany
*12	1940	Tokyo(gave up) / Helsinki-2	Japan/Finland				
*13	1944	London-3	UK				
14	1948	London	UK	5	1948	St. Moritz	Switzerland
15	1952	Helsinki	Finland	6	1952	Oslo	Norway
16	1956	Melbourne/ Stockholm	Australia/ Sweden	7	1956	Cortina d'Ampezzo	Italy
17	1960	Rome	Italy	8	1960	Squaw Valley	USA
18	1964	Tokyo	Japan	9	1964	Innsbruck	Austria
19	1968	Mexico	Mexico	10	1968	Grenoble	France
20	1972	Munich	Germany	11	1972	Sapporo	Japan
21	1976	Montreal	Canada	12	1976	Innsbruck	Austria
22	1980	Moscow	Russia	13	1980	Lake Placid	USA
23	1984	Los Angeles	USA	14	1984	Sarajevo	Yugoslavia
24	1988	Seoul	Korea	15	1988	Calgary	Canada
25	1992	Barcelona	Spain	16	1992	Albertville	France
				17	1994	Lillehammer	Norway
26	1996	Atlanta	USA				
				18	1998	Nagano	Japan
27	2000	Sydney	Australia				
				19	2002	Salt Lake City	USA
28	2004	Athens	Greece				
				20	2006	Turin	Italy
29	2008	Beijing	China				
				21	2010	Vancouver	Canada
30	2012	London	UK				
				22	2014	Sochi	Russia

Chapter 9
Useful Information

9-1 Hotels and Inns

Beijing Hotel 

33 Dong Chang'an Jie, Dongcheng District

86-10-6513-7766

www.chinabeijinghotel.com.cn

Kunlun Hotel Beijing 

2 Xinyuan Nan Lu, Chaoyang District

86-10-6590-3388

www.hotelkunlun.com

Beijing Kepinski Hotel 

50 Liangmaqiao Lu, Chaoyang District

86-10-6465-3388

www.kempinski-beijing.com

Zhao Long Hotel Beijing ★★★★★

2 Gongti Bei Lu, Chaoyang District

86-10-6597-2299

www.zhaolonghotel.com.cn

Grand Hyatt Beijing ★★★★★

1 Dong Chang'an Jie, Dongcheng District

86-10-8518-1234

beijing.grand hyatt.com

Grand Hotel Beijing ★★★★★

35 Dong Chang'an Jie, Dongcheng District

86-10-6513-7788

www.grandhotelbeijing.com

Peninsula ★★★★★

8 Jinyu Hutong, Wangfujing, Dongcheng District

86-10-8615-2888

www.peninsula.com

Hotel New Otani Chang Fu Gong ★★★★★

26 Jianguomenwai Da Jie, Chaoyang District

86-10-6512-5555

www.cfgbj.com

The St. Regis Beijing ★★★★★

21 Jianguomenwai Da Jie, Dongcheng District

86-10-6460-6688

www.stregis.com/beijing

Xiyuan Hotel ★★★★★

1 Sanlihe Lu, Haidian District

86-10-6831-3388

www.xiyuanhotel.com.cn

Beijing News Plaza Hotel ★★★★★

26 Jianguomennei Da Jie, Dongcheng District
86-10-6521-1188
www. newsplaza.com.cn

Marco Polo Hotel Beijing

78 Anli Road, Chaoyang District
86-10-5963-6688
www.marcopolohotels.com

Landmark Towers ★★★★

8 Dongsanhuan Bei Lu, Chaoyang District
80-10-6590-6688
www.beijinglandmark.com

CTS Hotel Beijing ★★★★

2 Bei Sanhuan Dong Lu, Chaoyang District
80-10-6462-2288
www.ctshotel.com

Capital Hotel ★★★★

3 Qianmen Dong Da Jie, Chongwen District
86-10-6512-9988
www.capitalhotel.com.cn

The North Garden ★★★★

281-1 Wangfujing Da Jie, Dongcheng District
86-10-6523-8888
www.north-garden.com

Zhongyu Century Grand Hotel ★★★★

31 Lianhua Dong Lu, Haidian District
86-10-6398-9999
www.zhongyuhotel.com.cn

Gloria Plaza Hotel Beijing ★★★★

2 Jianguomen Nan Da Jie, Chaoyang District
86-10-6515-8855
www.gloriahotels.com

Rosedale Hotel & Suites Beijing ★★★★

8 Jiangtai Xi Lu, Chaoyang District
86-10-5960-2288
www.rosedalebj.com

Sino-Swiss Hotel Beijing Airport ★★★★

9 Xiao Tianzhu Lu, Capital International Airport
86-10-6456-5588
www.sino-swisshotel.com

International Youth Hostel -China Lama Temple Youth Hostel

56 Beixinqiaotoutiao, Yonghegong Da Jie, Dongcheng District
86-10-6402-8663
www.hostelbeijing.com.cn

Peking Youth Hostel

5 Beichizi Er Tiao, Dongcheng District
86-10-6526-8855
www.pekinghostel.com.cn

Beijing Vanilla Garden International Youth Hostel

Hongdao Village, Machikou Town, Changping District
86-10-6077-2020
www.fcyc.com.cn

Far East International Youth Hostel

90 Tieshu Xie Jie, Xuanwu District
86-10-5195-8811
www.fareastyh.com

Beijing Lusongyuan Hotel

22 Banchang Hutong, Kuan Jie, Dongccheng District
86-10-6404-0436

Beijing Zhaolong Youth Hotel

2 Gongti Bei Lu, Chaoyang District
86-10- 6597-2299/6111

Beijing Shijia Youth Hostel

9 Shijia Hutong, Dongcheng District
86-10-6527-2773

Beijing Ruihaimu Youth Hostel

Ruihaimu Garden Resorts, Miyun County
86-10-8909-8888/8818

Beijing Drum Tower Youth Hostel

51 Jiu Gulou Da Jie, Xicheng District
86-10-6403-7702
www.guyunhostel.com

Home Inn

Today, Home Inn is China's largest chain of hotels. The founders of Home Inn have largely focused on the enormous expansion of this franchise. Although not recognized as a five-star hotel, Home Inn is absolutely affordable and very well looked after.

Addess	District	Tel: 86-10	Price(CNY)
1 Nanyixiang, Sanlihe	Xicheng	6851-3131	247-359
3 Yongxiag Hutong, Xizhimen	Xicheng	6611-1166	299
67 Ande Lu	Xicheng	8202-2828	219-239
61 Liangshidian Jie, Qianmen	Xuanwu	6317-3366	200-400
13 Xijing Lu	Xuanwu	8315-2266	239-299
71 Dongheyan	Xuanwu	5123-2266	259
16 Shuangqing Lu	Haidian	8241-1980	199-219
21 East 3rd Ring Road, Zhong Lu	Haidian	6397-1199	299-589
A3 Zizhuyuan Lu	Haidian	6841-6688	279
11 Shangdichangye Lu	Haidian	6296-2299	199-219
8 Xinyuan Nan Lu	Chaoyang	6597-1866	299-580
20 Baiziwan Lu	Chaoyang	8771-1155	259-299
17 Buiding, Tuanjiehu Lu	Chaoyang	8598-2266	219-359
48 East 3rd Ring Road (Nan Lu)	Chaoyang	6778-6633	199-279
A 78 Beiyuan Lu, Anwai	Chaoyang	8493-9933	199-299
A 52 Anli Lu	Chaoyang	8480-2999	239-279
1 Fangzhuang Lu	Fengtai	6762-5566	219-259
4 Xiaotun Lu	Fengtai	6869-5588	199
14 South 3rd Ring Road	Fengtai	6346-8788	179-199
A 29 Feng Bei Lu	Fengtai	5220-1212	199-259

9-2 Foreign Embassies

Country	Address of Embassy	Tel(86-10)
Afghanistan	8 Dongzhimenwai Da Jie	6532-1582
Albania	28 Guanghua Lu	6532-1120
Algeria	7 Sanlitun Lu	6532-1231
Austria	5 Xiushui Nan Jie,Jianguomenwai	6532-2061
Argentina	11 Sanlitun Dong Wu Jie	6532-1406
Australia	21 Dongzhimenwai Da Jie	6532-2331
Brazil	27 Guanghua Lu	6532-2881
Bulgaria	4 Xiushui Bei Jie,Jianguomenwai	6532-1946
Bolivia	2-3-2 Tayuan Diplomatic Building	6532-3074
Bangladesh	42 Guanghua Lu	6532-2521
Cambodia	9 Dongzhimenwai Da Jie	6532-1889
Canada	19 Dongzhimenwai Da Jie	6532-3536
Chile	1 Sanlitun Dong Si Jie	6532-1591
Cuba	1 Xiushui Nan Jie,Jianguomenwai	6532-6568
Central African Republic	1-1-132 Tayuan Diplomatic Building	6532-7353
Colombia	34 Guanghua Lu	6532-3377
Croatia	2-72 Sanlitun Diplomatic Building	6532-6241
Cameroon	7 Sanlitun Dong Wu Jie	6532-1828
Denmark	1 Sanlitun Dong Wu Jie	8532-9900
Dominica	LA06 Liangmaqiao Diplomatic Building	6532-0838
D.P.R. of Korea	11 Ritan Bei Lu	6532-1186
Egypt	2 Ritan Dong Lu	6532-1825
France	3 Sanlitun Dong San Jie	8532-8080
Finland	Level 26 South Tower Kerry Centre,Guanghua Lu	8519-8300
Greece	19 Guanghua Lu	6532-1317
Germany	17 Dongzhimenwai Da Jie	8532-9000
Hungary	10 Dongzhimenwai Da jie	6532-1431
Iraq	25 Xiushui Bei Jie,Jianguomenwai	6532-3385
Iran	13 Sanlitun Dong Liu Jie	6532-2040
Indonesia	4 Dongzhimenwai Da Jie	6532-5488
Israel	17 Tianze Lu	8532-0500
India	1 Ritan Dong Lu	6532-1856
Italy	2 Sanlitun Dong Er Jie	8532-7600
Ireland	No.3 Ritan Dong Lu	6532-2691
Japan	7 Ritan Lu,Jianguomenwai	6532-2361
Jamaica	6-2-72 Diplomatic Compound,1 Xiushui Street	6532-0670

CONTINUE

Country	Address of Embassy	Tel(86-10)
Kuwait	23 Guanghua Lu	6532-2216
Kenya	4 Sanlitun Xi Liu Jie	6532-3381
Korea	20 Dongfang Dong Lu	8531-0700
Laos	11 Sanlitun Dong Si Jie	6532-1224
Lebanon	10 Sanlitun Dong Liu Jie	6532-1560
Libya	3 Sanlitun Dong Liu Jie	6532-3666
Liberia	Room 013,No.1 Xibahe Nanlu	6440-3007
Luxembourg	21 Neiwubu Jie	6513-5937
Malaysia	2 Liangmaqiao Bei Jie	6532-2531
Mongolia	2 Xiushui Bei Jie,Jianguomenwai	6532-1203
Mexico	5 Sanlitun Dong Wu Jie	6532-2574
Netherlands	4 Liangmahe Nan Lu	6532-1131
Nepal	1 Sanlitun Xi Liu Jie	6532-1795
Nigeria	2 Sanlitun Dong Wu Jie	6532-3631
New Zealand	1 Ritan Dong Er Jie	6532-2731
Norway	1 Sanlitun Dong Yi Jie	6532-2261
Pakistan	1 Dongzhimenwai Da Jie	6532-2504
Philippines	23 Xiushui Bei Jie,Jianguomenwai	6532-1872
Peru	1-91 Sanlitun Office Building	6532-3719
Poland	1 Ritan Lu,Jianguomenwai	6532-1235
Portugal	8 Sanlitun Dong Wu Jie	6532-3497
Palestine	2 Sanlitun Dong San Jie	6532-1361
Russia	4 Dongzhimennei Bei Zhong Jie	6532-2051
Singapore	1 Xiushui Bei jie,Jianguomenwai	6532-1115
Syria	6 Sanlitun Dong Si Jie	6532-1372
Saudi Arabia	1 Sanlitun Bei Xiao Jie	6532-5325
South Africa	5 Dongzhimenwai Da Jie	6532-0171
Sweden	3 Dongzhimenwai Da Jie	6532-9790
Switzerland	3 Sanlitun Dong Wu Jie	8532-8888
Spain	9 Sanlitun Lu	6532-1986
Thailand	40 Guanghua Lu	6532-1749
Turkey	9 Sanlitun Dong Wu Jie	6532-1715
U.S.A.	3 Xiushui Bei Jie,Jianguomenwai	6532-3831
U.K.	11 Guanghua Lu	5192-4000
Vietnam	32 Guanghua Lu,Jianguomenwai	6532-1155

9-3 Office of International Organizations

Offices of Organizations of the United Nations System

2 Liangmahe Nan Lu, Chaoyang District
86-10-6532-3731

United Nations Development Program (UNDP)

2 Liangmahe Nan Lu, Chaoyang District
86-10-8532-0800

Food and Agriculture Organization of the United Nations (FAO)

4-2, 151 Diplomatic Building, Jianguomenwai Da Jie, Chaoyang District
86-10-6532-5042

United Nations Population Fund

2 Liangmahe Nan Lu, Chaoyang District
86-10-6532-3733

United Nations Children's Fund

12 Sanlitun Lu, Chaoyang District
86-10-6532-3131

World Health Organization (WHO)

401 Dongwai Diplomatic Building, 23 Dongzhimenwai Da Jie, Chaoyang District
86-10-6532-7189

United Nations Educational, Scientific and Cultural Organization (UNESCO)

153 Building 5, Jianguomenwai Da Jie, Chaoyang District
86-10-6532-1725

The World Bank Office, Beijing (WBOB)

18th Floor, China World Tower 2, Jianguomenwai Da Jie, Chaoyang District
86-10-5861-7701

International Monetary Fund

Room 3612, China Word Tower 2, 1 Jianguomenwai Da Jie, Chaoyang District

9-4 International Clinics

Peking Union Medical College Hospital, Foreigners' Emergency Clinic

53 Dongdan Bei Da Jie, Doncheng District

86-10-6529-5269

Sino-Japanese Friendship Hospital

Yinghua DongLu, Heping Jie Bei Kou, Chaoyang District

86-10-6422-2952

International Medical Center (IMC)

Room 5106, Beijing Lufthansa Center, 50 Liangmaqiao Lu, Chaoyang District

86-10-6465-1561/62/63

International SOS

Building C, BITIC Leasing Center, 1 Xingfu San Cun Bei Lu, Chaoyang District

86-10-6462-9112 for clinic apartment,86-10-6462-9100 for 24-hour alarm line, 86-10-6462—0555 for general information

Hong Kong International medical Clinic

9/F, Hong Kong Macau Center, 2 Chaoyangmen Bei Da Jie, Dong Cheng District

86-10-6553-2288, ext. 2345/2346/2347

Beijing United Family Hospital

2 Jiangtai Lu, Chaoyang District

86-10-6433-3961

Bayley & Jackson Medical group

7 Ritan Dong Lu, Chaoyang District

86-10-8562-9998

Guree Dental

NB 210, China World Trade Center, 1 Jianguomen Wai Da Jie, Chaoyang District

86-10-6505-9439

Wista Clinic

B29, Kerry Center, 1 Guanghua Lu, Chaoyang District

86-10-8529-6618

9-5 Tours and Travel Agencies

Beijing has plentiful tourist resources. More than 200 tourist hotspots are available to visitors from all over the world. About 456 travel agencies operate in Beijing, employing over 5,000 professional tourist guides, who are capable of speaking up to 21 languages. Most hotels usually offer excursions to the prominent sites, and the average cost of city tours is 300 CNY.

The list of tourist Companies offering service in Beijing:

Company Name	Telephone Number	Webpage
China International Travel Servie(CITS)	86-10-8522-8888	www.cits.cn/en/index.htm
Beijing Youth Travel Service Co.LTD.(BYTS)	86-10-6327-3113/2973	www.byts.com.cn
China Travel Service(CTS)	86-10-6462-2288	www.ctsho.com
China Civil International Tourist Corp.(CCITC)	86-10-6447-6615,8451-6616	www.ccitc.com.cn
China Women Travel Service	86-10-6523-1459	www.cwtstour.com
China Cultural International Tours Inc.		www.chinaculture.org
Tour Beijing	hotline:86-10-6716-0201 ext 1006,1007 Emergency Call(Mobile): 86-13520598855,13901312027(24 hours)	www.tour-beijing.com
Beijing Hutong Tour Co.,LTD	86-10-8403-6483 Reservation by phone:86-10-6615-9097/6612-3236/640-02787	www.hutongtour.com.cn
China Commercial International Travel Service	86-10-5166-0915/0925 Emergency call(Mobile):86-13910972927	www.beijingimpression.com
High Quality China Tours	86-10-8316-1875	www.hqchinatours.com
China Muslim Holiday	86-10-6397-3491/3492/4971	www.muslimholiday.cn
Beijing 2008 Olympics		www.beijing-2008-olympics.com
Travel China Guide	800-840-9555(call in USA)	www.travelchinaguide.com
McIntosh Tours		www.chinatour.com
My Beijing China	86-773-231-999	www.mybeijingchina.com
China Odyssey Tours	86-773-582-4466,583-0803	www.chinaodysseytours.com
The Beijing Page	email:sunny302@yahoo.com	www.beijingpage.com
China Highlights	86-773-2831-999(for all countries)	www.chinahighlights.com
Sino Way Travel	86-773-2887-305	www.beijingholiday.net
Oriental Travel		www.orientaltravel.com
Beijing Tourist Bureau	86-10-8515-7056	www.bjta.gov.cn

9-6 Airlines

Air Canada

✆ 888-247-2262 in North America
86-10-6468-2001 in China
Ⓦ www.aircanada.com

Air China

✆ 86-10-6466-1697 in China
Ⓦ www.airchina.com.cn

Air France

✆ 4008-808-808 in China
Ⓦ www.airfrance.com

Air Macau

✆ 86-10-6515-9398 in China
Ⓦ www.bj.sirmacau.com.cn

British Airways

✆ 0870-850-9850 in The U.K.
400-650-0073 in China
Ⓦ www.britishairways.com

Dragon Airlines

✆ 86-10-6518-2533 in China
Ⓦ www.dragonair.com

Japan Airlines

✆ 800-525-3663 in North America
400-888-0808 in China
Ⓦ www.jal.com

Korean Air

✆ 800-438-5000 in North America
86-10-8453-8421 in China
Ⓦ www.koreanair.com

NorthWest Airlines

800-225-2525 in North America
400-814-0081 in China

www.nwa.com

Qantas Airlines

02-9691-3636 in Australia
86-10-6567-9006 in China

www.qantas.com

United Airlines

800-864-8331 in North America
86-10-8468-6666 in China

www.united.com

Thai Airways International

10-8515-0088 in China

www.thaiair.com

All Nippon Airways

800-235-9262 in North America
10-6590-9177 in China

www.anaskyweb.com/us/e

9-7 Important Phone Numbers

Police Dispatch: 110
Medical Emergency: 120 or 999
Fire Dispatch: 119
Traffic Accident: 122
Weather Broadcast: 12121
Phone Number Inquiries: 114
Time Inquires: 12117
24-hour Tourist Hotline: 86–10–65130828

9-8 Water and Power Supply

Tap water in China is considered hard and need to be boiled before drinking.

China uses a 220–voltage power supply for standard, domestic, and business purposes.

9-9 (A) Beijing Airport Shuttle Buses Schedule

Route	Start	Stops										Final	First Bus/ Final Bus
1	Capital Airport	Liangmaqiao	Hujialou	Dabeiyao (Trade Centre)	Panjiayuan	Shilihe(KingWing Hot Spring) Internationanl Hotel						Fangzhauang (Guiyou Mall)	6:00/19:30
	Fang Zhuang (Guiyou Mail)	Dabeiyao(South China Aviation Hotel)										Capital Airport	7:30/22:30
2	Capital Airport	Sanyuanqiao	Dongzhimen	Dongsishitiao qiao								Xidan(Civil AviationBuilding)	7:00/Till the last Flight
	Xidan(Civil AviationBuilding)	Dongzhimen	JingxinBuilding(west entry)									Capital Airport	5:30/21:00
3	Capital Airport	Yuyang Hotel	Dongdaqiao(bypassed after 22:30)	Chaoyangmen	Yabao Lu							Beijing Railway Station	7:30/Till the last Flight
	Beijing Raiway Station	International Hotel(West Entry)	Dongzhimen(50m east of Bridge)	Jingxin Build(West Entry)								Capital Airport	5:30/21:00
4	Capital Airport	International Exhibition Centre	Xibahe	Anzhen Qiao	Madian Qiao	Beitaiping zhuang	Jimen Qiao	Firendship Hotel	Beijing TV Station	Zizhu Qiao	Hangtian Qiao	Gongzhufen (Xinxing Hotel)	7:00/23:00
	Gongzhufen	Gongzhufen(Xinxing Hotel)	Friendship Hotel(North Entry Air Ticket Office)	Beitaipingzhuang(50m east of the crossroad)	Anzhen Qiao							Capital Airport	5:30/21:00
5	Capital Airport	Wangjing(Huajiadi)	Xiaoying	Yayuncun (Anhuiqiao)	Xueyuanqiao							Zhongguan Cun Qiao	08:30/21:30
	Zhongguancun	Beihang University(North Entry)	Huixin Xi Jie(Anhui Qiao)	Huixin Dong Jie(Sinopec)								Capital Airport	6:00/19:30
6	Nanyuan Airport	Fuhai Park										Xidan	Operation hours: 12:40/17:10/20:50
	Xidan	Dahongmen Garments Wholesale Market										Nanyuan Airport	Operation hours: 6:00/10:40/15:10

9-9 (B) Airport Shuttle

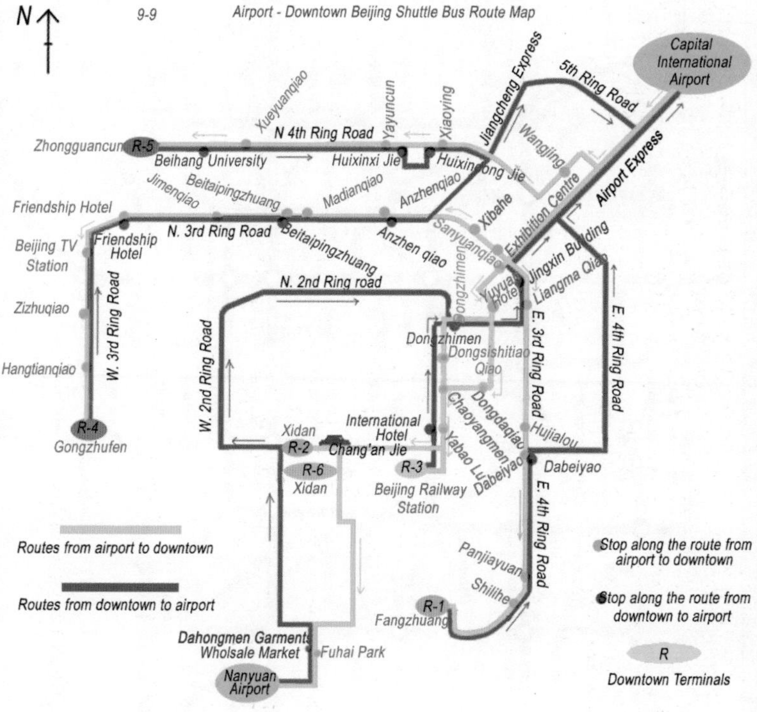

N

9-9 Airport - Downtown Beijing Shuttle Bus Route Map

Capital International Airport
5th Ring Road
Jiangcheng Express
Airport Express
Wangjing
Xiaoying
Yayuncun
Xueyuanqiao
N 4th Ring Road
Zhongguancun
R-5
Beihang University
Huixinxi Jie
Huixindong Jie
Jimenqiao
Beitaipingzhuang
Madianqiao
Anzhenqiao
Xibahe
Exhibition Centre
Friendship Hotel
N. 3rd Ring Road
Beitaipingzhuang
Anzhen qiao
Sanyuanqiao
Jingxin Building
Liangma Qiao
Beijing TV Station
Friendship Hotel
W. 3rd Ring Road
Zizhuqiao
Hangtianqiao
R-4
Gongzhufen
N. 2nd Ring road
Dongzhimen
Yuyuan Hotel
Dongzhimen
Dongsishitiao Qiao
E. 3rd Ring Road
E. 4th Ring Road
W. 2nd Ring Road
Dongdaqiao
Chaoyangmen
Yabao Lu
Hujialou
Dabeiyao
Dabeiyao
International Hotel
Xidan
R-2
Chang'an Jie
R-3
R-6
Xidan
Beijing Railway Station
E. 4th Ring Road
Panjiayuan
Shilihe
R-1
Fangzhuang
Dahongmen Garments Wholsale Market
Fuhai Park
Nanyuan Airport

Routes from airport to downtown

Routes from downtown to airport

Stop along the route from airport to downtown

Stop along the route from downtown to airport

R
Downtown Terminals

9-10 Beijing Subway

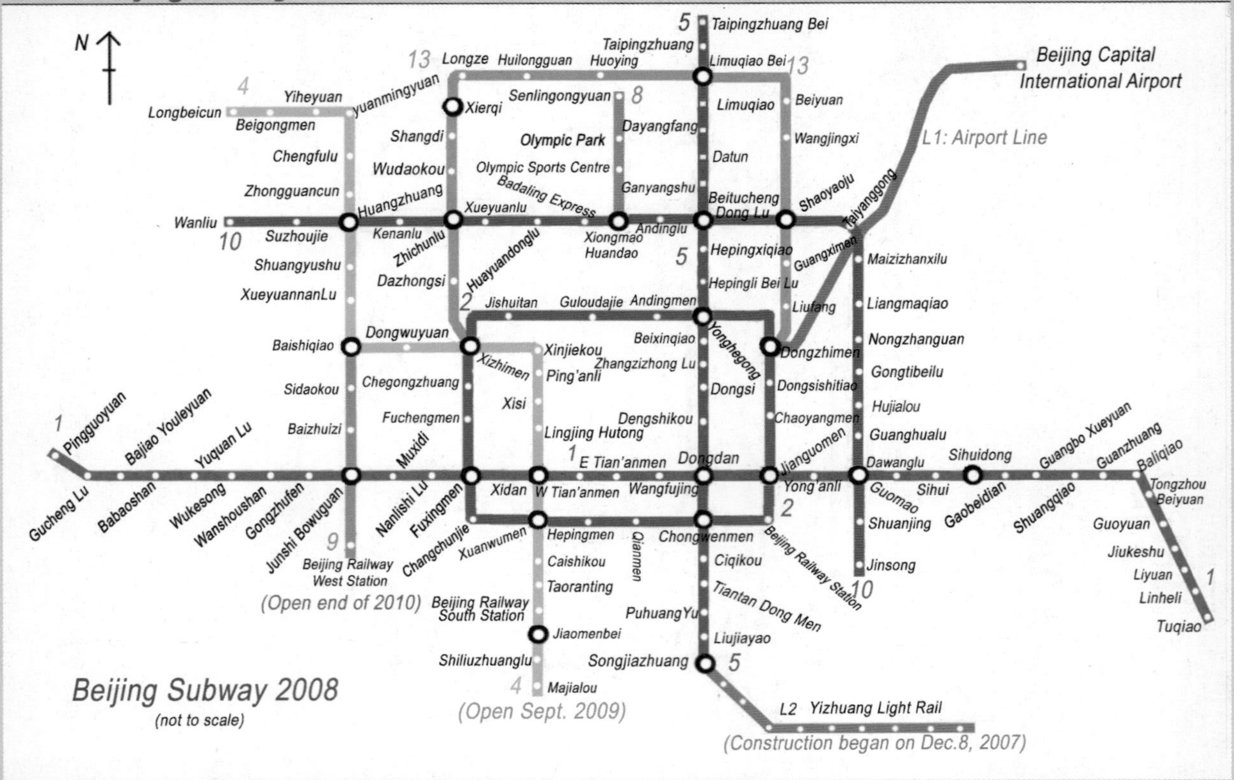

N

Beijing Subway 2008
(not to scale)

Beijing Capital International Airport
L1: Airport Line

5 Taipingzhuang Bei
Taipingzhuang
13 Longze Huilongguan Huoying
Limuqiao Bei 13
4 Longbeicun Yiheyuan yuanmingyuan
Beigongmen
Xierqi
Senlingongyuan 8
Limuqiao
Beiyuan
Shangdi
Olympic Park
Dayangfang
Wangjingxi
Chengfulu
Wudaokou
Olympic Sports Centre
Datun
Zhongguancun
Badaling Express
Ganyangshu
Huangzhuang
Xueyuanlu
Beitucheng
Dong Lu
Shaoyaoju
Taiyanggong
Wanliu 10
Suzhoujie
Kenanlu
Zhichunlu
Xiongmao Huandao
Andinglu
5
Hepingxiqiao
Guangximen
Maizizhanxilu
Shuangyushu
Huayuandonglu
Hepingli Bei Lu
XueyuannanLu
Dazhongsi
2 Jishuitan Guloudajie Andingmen
Liufang
Liangmaqiao
Dongwuyuan
Baishiqiao
Xizhimen
Xinjiekou
Beixinqiao
Zhangzizhong Lu
Yonghegong
Dongzhimen
Nongzhanguan
Sidaokou
Chegongzhuang
Ping'anli
Dongsi
Dongsishitiao
Gongtibeilu
Xisi
Hujialou
Fuchengmen
Dengshikou
Chaoyangmen
Baizhuizi
Lingjing Hutong
Guanghualu
1 Pingguoyuan
Bajiao Youleyuan
Yuquan Lu
Muxidi
1 E Tian'anmen
Dongdan
Jianguomen
Dawanglu
Sihuidong
Guangbo Xueyuan
Guanzhuang
Baliqiao
Gucheng Lu
Babaoshan
Wukesong
Wanshoushan
Gongzhufen
Junshi Bowuguan
Nanlishi Lu
Fuxingmen
Xidan
W Tian'anmen
Wangfujing
Yong'anli
Guomao
Sihui
Gaobeidian
Shuangqiao
Tongzhou Beiyuan
2
Guoyuan
9
Changchunjie
Xuanwumen
Hepingmen
Qianmen
Chongwenmen
Beijing Railway Station
Shuanjing
Jiukeshu
Beijing Railway West Station
Caishikou
Ciqikou
Jinsong
Liyuan
(Open end of 2010)
Taoranting
Tiantan Dong Men
10
1
Linheli
Beijing Railway South Station
PuhuangYu
Tuqiao
Jiaomenbei
Liujiayao
Shiliuzhuanglu
Songjiazhuang 5
4 Majialou
(Open Sept. 2009)
L2 Yizhuang Light Rail
(Construction began on Dec.8, 2007)

Chapter 10

Basic Conversation in Chinese

Chinese or Mandarin use Pinyin to pronounce Chinese words. Pinyin is written in Roman alphabet. There are a few consonants in Pinyin that are different from English.

c	as the "ts" in "bits"
ch	like "ch" in "chin", but with the tongue curled upward
q	as the "ch" in "church".
r	like "r" in "rank"
sh	as "sh" in "shipping", but with the tongue curled upward
x	like "C" in "A B C"
z	like sound in "zap"
zh	like "dr" in "draw", but with the tongue curled upward

10-1 Basic Conversation, Greetings and Introductions

Hello!	你好！	ni hao
How are you?	你好吗？	ni hao ma ?
I'm fine.	我还好。	wo hai hao.
Good morning!	早上好!	zao shang hao!

Good evening!	晚上好！	wan shang hao!
Please.	请。	qing.
Thank you!	谢谢！	xie xie!
You're welcome.	不客气。	bu ke qi.
Sorry.	对不起。	dui bu qi.
It's ok!	没关系！	mei guan xi!
Goodbye!	再见！	zai jian!
See you tomorrow.	明天见。	ming tian jian.
Good night.	晚安。	wan an.
Good luck.	祝你好运。	zhu ni hao yun.
What is your name?	叫什么名字？	ni jiao shen me ming zi?
My name is....	我叫	wo jiao ......
Where are you from?	你从哪儿来？	ni cong na er lai ?
I'm American.	我是美国人。	wo shi mei guo ren.
Sorry, I don't understand.	对不起，我听不懂。	dui bu qi, wo ting bu dong.
Thank you.	谢谢你。	xie xie.

10-2 Number, Date, Time and Direction

One	一	yi
Two	二	er
Three	三	san
Four	四	si
Five	五	wu
Six	六	liu
Seven	七	qi
Eight	八	ba
Nine	九	jiu
Ten	十	shi
Hundred	百	bai
Thousand	千	qian
Million	百万	bai wan
Monday	星期一	xing qi yi

Tuesday	星期二	xing qi er
Wednesday	星期三	xing qi san
Thursday	星期四	xing qi si
Friday	星期五	xing qi wu
Saturday	星期六	xing qi liu
Sunday	星期日 / 天	xing qi ri/tian
Today	今天	jin tian
Yesterday	昨天	zuo tian
Tomorrow	明天	ming tian
Morning	上午	shang wu
Noon	中午	zhong wu
Afternoon	下午	xia wu
Evening	晚上	wan shang
1 O'clock	一点	yi dian
2 O'clock	两点	liang dian
3:05 pm	下午三点五分	xia wu san dian wu fen
10:45 am	上午十点四十五分	shang wu shi dian si shi wu fen
What day is today?	今天星期几？	Jin tian xing qi ji ?
Today is Wednesday.	今天星期三。	Jin tian xin qi san.
What time is it?	现在几点？	Xian zai ji dian ?
It's 1:08pm.	下午一点零八分。	Xia wu yi dian ling ba fen.
East	东	dong
South	南	nan
West	西	xi
North	北	bei
Up	上	shang
Down	下	xia
Left	左	zuo
Right	右	you

10-3 In Customs

Where are you from?
你从哪里来？/ Ni cong na li lai?

I'm from America.
我从美国来。 / Wo cong mei guo lai.

What is the purpose of your visit?
你的旅行目的是什么？ / Ni de lü xing mu di shi shen mo?

Sightseeing.
观光。 / Guan guang.

How long will you stay?
打算停留多久？ / Da suan ting liu duo jiu?

I will stay for two weeks.
两个星期。 / Liang ge xing qi.

I have nothing to declare.
我没有东西要申报。 / Wo mei you dong xi yao shen bao.

International	国际	guo ji
Domestic	国内	guo nei
E-ticket	电子机票	dian zi ji piao
Customs declaration form	入境申报单	ru jing shen bao dan
Medicine	药物	yao wu
Cigarette	香烟	Xiang yan
Liquor	酒	jiu
Perfume	香水	Xiang shui
Gift	礼品	li pin
Passport	护照	hu zhao
Visa	签证	qian zheng
Quarantine	检疫	jian yi

Immigration	入境检查	ru jing jian cha
Carry-on luggage	手提行李	shou ti xing li
Duty free	免税	mian shui

10-4 Currency Exchange

I would like to change some money.
我想换钱。 / Wo xiang huan qian.

What is today's exchange rate?
今天的汇率是多少？ / Jin tian de hui lü shi duo shao?

6.75 RMB for 1 dollar
1 美元换 6.75 元人民币。/ Yi mei yuan huan Liu dian qi wu yuan ren min bi.

Please get me a taxi.
请叫出租车。/ Qing jiao chu zu che.

This is tip.
这是小费。/ Zhe shi xiao fei.

Bank	银行	yin hang
Foreign currency	外汇	wai hui
Renminbi (RMB)	人民币	ren min bi
Bill	纸币	zhi bi
Coin	硬币	ying bi
Yuan	元	yuan
Jiao	角	jiao
Fen	分	fen
Exchange rate	汇率	hui lü
Taxi	出租车	chu zu che
How much	多少钱	duo shao qian
Driver	司机	si ji

10-5 In Hotel

Do you have a room available tonight?
今晚有房间吗？/ Jin wan you fang jian ma?

Have you made a reservation?
你预约了吗？ / Ni yu yue le ma?

No, I do not have a reservation.
没有预约。/ Mei you yu yue.

What kind of room do you want?
你要什么样的房间？/ Ni yao shen me yang de fang jian?

A double room with bath, please.
带浴室的双人房间。/ Dai yu shi de shuang ren fang jian.

580RMB per night.
580 元钱一个晚上。 / Wu bai ba shi yuan yi ge wan shang.

Elevator is in left side and restaurant is in the 15th floor.
电梯在左边，餐厅在 15 楼。/ Dian ti zai zuo bian, can ting zai shi wu lou.

How to make an international call?
怎么打国际长途电话？/ Zen me da guo ji chang tu dian hua?

We are leaving today so we want to check out.
我们今天离开，现在退房。/ Wo men jin tian li kai, xian zai tui fang.

Front desk	前台	qian tai
Reservation	预约	yu yue
Single room	单人房间	dan ren fang jian
Double room	双人房间	shuan ren fang jian
Suite room	套间	tao jian
Key	钥匙	yao shi
Elevator	电梯	dian ti

Bath room	浴室	yu shi
Soap	肥皂	fei zao
Towel	毛巾	mao jin
TV	电视	dian shi
Wireless Internet	无线网	wu xian wang
Telephone	电话	dian hua
Restaurant	餐厅	can ting
Coffee bar	咖啡厅	ka fei ting
Bar	酒吧	jiu bar
Gift shop	小卖部	xiao mai bu
Emergency exit	紧急出口	jin ji chu kou

10-6 Sightseeing

How can I get to Badaling Great Wall?
去八达岭长城怎么走？/ Qu ba da ling chang cheng zen me zou?

We will go to the Summer Palace tomorrow.
我们明天去颐和园。/ Wo men ming tian qu yi he yuan.

I want to go to Beijing Capital International Airport.
我要去首都机场。/ Wo yao qu shou du ji chang.

The train has been delayed.
火车晚点了。 / Huo che wan dian le.

Where is the ticket office?
售票处在哪儿？/ Shou piao chu zai na er?

Airplane	飞机	fei ji
Train	火车	huo che
Subway	地铁	di tie
Bus	公共汽车	gong gong qi che
Taxi	出租车	chu zu che

Sightseeing boat	游览船	you lan chuan
Airport	机场	ji chang
Station	车站	che zhan
Port	轮船码头	lun chuan ma tou
Ticket	机票，车票	ji piao, che piao
Timetable	时刻表	shi ke biao
Guide	导游	dao you
Museum	博物馆	bo wu guan
Art Gallery	美术馆	mei shu guan
Theater	剧场 / 电影院	ju chang/dian ying yuan
Temple	寺庙	si miao
Park	公园	gong yuan
Bridge	桥	qiao

10-7 Shopping

How much is it?
这个多少钱？/ Zhe ge duo shao qian?

It is too expensive. Can it be cheaper?
太贵了，能便宜点吗? / Tai gui le ,neng pian yi dian ma?

Can I see another one?
能让我看看另外一个吗？/ Neng rang wo kan kan ling wai yi ge ma?

Do you have one like this?
你有和这个一样的吗？/ Ni you he zhe ge yi yang de ma?

I like this one.
我喜欢这一个。/ Wo xi huan zhe yi ge.

I want to buy one in Large Size.
我买一件大号的。/ Wo mai yi jian da hao de.

Do you accept credit card?
能用信用卡付款吗？/ Neng yong xin yong ka fu kuan ma?

Market	市场	shi chang
Department store	百货商场	bai huo shang chang
Supermarket	超级市场	chao ji shi chang
Flea-market	跳蚤市场	tiao zao shi chang
Duty free shop	免税店	mian shui dian
Craft shop	工艺美术商店	gong yi mei shu shang dian
Gift shop	礼品店	li pin dian
Fashion shop	时装店	shi zhuang dian
Convenience store	小卖店	xiao mai dian
Credit card	信用卡	xin yong ka
Traveler check	旅行支票	lü xing zhi piao
Cash	现金	xian jin

10-8 Restaurant

I like Chinese food.
我喜欢吃中餐。/ Wo xi huan chi zhong can.

What would you like?
想吃什么？/ Xiang chi shen me?

Let us go to have some Beijing roast duck.
我们去吃北京烤鸭吧。/ Wo men qu chi Beijing kao ya ba.

This is menu. What kind of drink do you like?
这是菜单，想喝点什么吗？/ Zhe shi cai dan, Xiang he dian shen me ma?

Shall we order now?
我们点菜吧？ / Wo men dian cai ba?

What is this? This dish, please.
这是什么？我要这个菜。 / Zhe shi shen me? Wo yao zhe ge cai.

Do not make it too hot.
不要太辣。/ Bu yao tai la.

This soup is too oily.
这个汤很油。/ Zhe ge tang hen you.

Do you want some dessert?
要甜点吗？/ Yao tian dian ma?

I am full.
吃饱了。/ Chi bao le.

Breakfast	早餐	zao can
Lunch	午餐	wu can
Dinner	晚餐	wan can
Chinese restaurant	中餐馆	zhong can guan
Western style restaurant	西餐馆	xi can guan
French food	法国餐	fa guo can
Italian food	意大利餐	yi da li can
Japanese food	日本餐	ri ben can
MacDonald	麦当劳	mai dang lao
KFC	肯德基	ken de ji
Pizza	比萨饼	bi sa bing
Light	清淡	qing dan
Oily	油腻	you ni
Hot	辣	la

What would you like to drink?
您喝点什么？ / Nin he dian shen me?

Orange juice please.
请给我一杯橘子汁。/ Qing gei wo yi bei ju zi zhi.

10-9 Illness, Emergency

I am sick.
我生病了。/ Wo sheng bing le.

I have a bad headache. Please call a doctor.
我头痛，请叫医生。/ Wo tou tong, qing jiao yi sheng.

Please take me to the hospital nearby.
请带我去附近的医院。/ Qing dai wo qu fu jin de yi yuan.

Where does it hurt?
你哪儿疼？/ Ni na er teng?

You have a fever.
你发烧了。/ Ni fa shao le.

I have diarrhea.
我拉肚子。/ Wo la du zi.

Is there a pharmacy store?
哪儿有药店？/ Na er you yao dian?

I'm lost.
我迷路了。/ Wo mi lu le.

I injured myself.
我受伤了。/ Wo shou shang le.

I lost my wallet.
我钱包丢了。/ Wo qian bao diu le.

Headache	头疼	tou teng
Cold	感冒	gan mao
Fever	发烧	fa shao

Cough	咳嗽	ke sou
Diarrhea	拉肚子	la du zi
Head	头	tou
Eye	眼睛	yan jing
Nose	鼻子	bi zi
Ear	耳朵	er duo
Tooth	牙齿	ya chi
Tongue	舌头	she tou
Hand	手	shou
Foot	脚	jiao
Finger	手指	shou zhi
Toe	脚趾	jiao zhi
Chest	胸	xiong
Waist	腰	yao
Back	背	bei
Heart	心脏	xin zang
Lung	肺	fei
Stomach	胃	wei

10-10 Olympic Related Conversation and Words

Beijing welcomes you.
北京欢迎你。/ Beijing huan ying ni.

We want to go to Beijing to watch Olympic games.
我们想去北京看奥运会。/ Wo men xiang qu Beijing kan ao yun hui.

Where are the basketball games?
篮球比赛在哪儿举行？ / Lan qiu bi sai zai na er ju xing?

How can I get to Wukesong Stadium?
去五棵松体育馆怎么走？ / Qu wu ke song ti yu guan zen mo zou?

Field and track games	田径赛	tian jing sai
Field games	田赛	tian sai
Track games	径赛	jing sai
Marathon	马拉松	ma la song
Hurdles	跨栏	kua lan
Relay	接力	jie li
Race walking	竞走	jing zou
Hammer throw	链球	lian qiu
Javelin throw	标枪	biao qiang
Discus throw	铁饼	tie bing
Shot put	铅球	qian qiu
High jump	跳高	tiao gao
Pole vault	撑竿跳高	cheng gan tiao gao
Long jump	跳远	tiao yuan
Triple jump	三级跳远	san ji tiao yuan
Triathlon	铁人三项	tie ren san xiang
Modern pentathlon	现代五项	xian dai wu xiang
Football	足球	zu qiu
Basketball	篮球	lan qiu
Volleyball	排球	pai qiu
Tennis	网球	wang qiu
Baseball	棒球	bang qiu
Softball	垒球	lei qiu
Hockey	曲棍球	qu gun qiu
Ice hockey	冰球	bing qiu
Water polo	水球	shui qiu
Handball	手球	shou qiu
Badminton	羽毛球	yu mao qiu
Table tennis	乒乓球	ping pang qiu
Gymnastics	体操	ti cao
Artistic gymnastics	艺术体操	yi shu ti cao
Swimming	游泳	you yong
Crawl stroke	蛙泳	wa yong
Butterfly stroke	蝶泳	die yong

Backstroke	仰泳	yang yong
Free style stroke	自由泳	zi you yong
Diving	跳水	tiao shui
Platform diving	跳台跳水	tiao tai tiao shui
Springboard diving	跳板跳水	tiao ban tiao shui
Canoe/Kayak	皮划艇	pi hua ting
Rowing	赛艇	sai ting
Sailing	帆船	fan chuan
Weightlifting	举重	ju zhong
Wrestling	摔跤	shuai jiao
Judo	柔道	rou dao
Taekwondo	跆拳道	tai quan dao
Boxing	拳击	quan ji
Fencing	击剑	ji jian
Shooting	射击	she ji
Archery	射箭	she jian
Cycling	自行车	zi xing che
Equestrian	马术	ma shu

责任编辑：王　军
责任印制：冯冬青

图书在版编目（CIP）数据

北京旅游手册＝Beijing Tourism Manual: 英文 /（美）王未江编. —北京：中国旅游出版社，2008.7
ISBN 978-7-5032-3484-2

Ⅰ.北…　Ⅱ.王…　Ⅲ.旅游指南—北京市—英文　Ⅳ.K928.91

中国版本图书馆CIP数据核字（2008）第092424号

书　　名：Beijing Tourism Manual
作　　者：Mier W. Wang
出版发行：中国旅游出版社
（北京建国门内大街甲9号　邮编：100005）
http://www.cttp.net.cn　E-mail:cttp@cnta.gov.cn
发行部电话：010-85166507　85166517
制　　版：北京中文天地文化艺术有限公司
经　　销：全国各地新华书店
印　　刷：北京金吉士印刷有限责任公司
版　　次：2008年7月第1版　2008年7月第1次印刷
开　　本：880毫米×1168毫米　1/32
印　　张：6.25
印　　数：1—5000册
字　　数：100千字
定　　价：50.00元
I S B N　978-7-5032-3484-2